JUNGLE DO

Africa

⑦

JUNGLE DOCTOR'S
Africa

Paul White

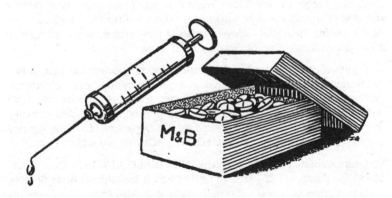

CF4·K

10 9 8 7 6 5 4 3 2

Jungle Doctor's Africa previously published as *Jungle Doctor*
ISBN 978-1-84550-388-8
© Copyright 1942 Paul White
First published 1942, reprinted 1950, 1951, 1952, 1953, 1954, 1955,
1957, 1958, 1960, 1963, 1965
Paperback edition 1972

Published in 2008 and reprinted in 2011
by Christian Focus Publications,
Geanies House, Fearn, Tain, Ross-shire, IV20 1TW, Scotland, U.K.
Fact files: © Copyright Christian Focus Publications
Paul White Productions,
4/1-5 Busaco Road, Marsfield, NSW 2122, Australia

Cover design: Daniel van Straaten
Cover illustration: Craig Howarth
Interior illustrations: Joy Griffin
Printed and Bound in Denmark by Nørhaven Paperback

*Since the Jungle Doctor books were first published there have been a
number of Jungle Doctors working in Mvumi Hospital, Tanzania, East
Africa - some Australian, some British, a West Indian and a number of
East African Jungle Doctors to name but a few.*

Scripture quotations taken from the HOLY BIBLE, NEW INTERNATIONAL
VERSION. Copyright © 1973, 1978, 1984 by International Bible Society.
Used by permission of Hodder & Stoughton Publishers.

Some Scripture quotations are based on the King James Version of the
Bible.

African words are used throughout the book, but explained at least once
within the text. A glossary is also included at the front of the book along
with a key character index.

Contents

Fact File: Paul White

Born in 1910 in Bowral, New South Wales, Australia, Paul had Africa in his blood for as long as he could remember. His father captured his imagination with stories of his experiences in the Boer War which left an indelible impression. His father died of meningitis in army camp in 1915, and he was left an only child without his father at five years of age. He inherited his father's storytelling gift along with a mischievous sense of humour.

He committed his life to Christ as a sixteen-year-old school-boy and studied medicine as the next step towards missionary work in Africa. Paul and his wife, Mary, left Sydney, with their small son, David, for Tanganyika in 1938. He always thought of this as his life's work but Mary's severe illness forced their early return to Sydney in 1941. Their daughter, Rosemary, was born while they were overseas.

Within weeks of landing in Sydney Paul was invited to begin a weekly radio broadcast which spread throughout Australia as the Jungle Doctor Broadcasts - the last of these was aired in 1985. The weekly scripts for these programmes became the raw material for the Jungle Doctor hospital stories - a series of twenty books.

Paul always said he preferred life to be a 'mixed grill' and so it was: writing, working as a Rheumatologist, public speaking, involvement with many Christian organisations, adapting the fable stories into multiple forms (comic books, audio cassettes, filmstrips), radio and television, and sharing his love of birds with others by producing bird song cassettes - and much more.

The books in part or whole have been translated into 109 languages.

Paul saw that although his plan to work in Africa for life was turned on its head, in God's better planning he was able to reach more people by coming home than by staying. It was a great joy to meet people over the years who told him they were on their way overseas to work in mission because of the books.

Paul's wife, Mary, died after a long illness in 1970. He married Ruth and they had the joy of working together on many new projects. He died in 1992 but the stories and fables continue to attract an enthusiastic readership of all ages.

Fact File: Tanzania

The Jungle Doctor books are based on Paul White's missionary experiences in Tanzania. Today many countries in Africa have gained their independence. This has resulted in a series of name changes. Tanganyika is one such country that has now changed its name to Tanzania.

The name Tanganyika is no longer used formally for the territory. Instead the name Tanganyika is used almost exclusively to mean the lake.

During World War I, what was then Tanganyika came under British military rule. On December 9, 1961 it became independent. In 1964, it joined with the island of Zanzibar to form the United Republic of Tanganyika and Zanzibar, changed later in the year to the United Republic of Tanzania.

It is not only its name that has changed, this area of Africa has gone through many changes since the *Jungle Doctor* books were first written. Africa itself has changed. Many of the same diseases raise their heads, but treatments have advanced. However new diseases come to take their place and the work goes on.

Missions throughout Africa are often now run by African Christians and not solely by foreign nationals. There are still the same problems to overcome however. The message of the gospel thankfully never changes and brings hope to those who listen and obey. *The Jungle Doctor* books are about this work to bring health and wellbeing to Africa as well as the good news of Jesus Christ and salvation.

Fact File: Meningitis

Meningitis is an inflammation of the membranes covering the brain and spinal cord, known as the meninges. Meningitis develops after contact with bacteria, viruses and other infectious agents, but can also be a result of physical injury, cancer, or certain drugs. While some forms of meningitis are mild it is a potentially serious condition. The potential for serious brain damage or even death means that medical attention is necessary. Meningitis is normally treated with antibiotics but some forms may be prevented with immunization.

A severe headache is the most common symptom followed by neck stiffness. The patient generally suffers from a sudden high fever and an altered mental status. Other signs commonly associated with meningitis are photophobia (inability to tolerate bright light), phonophobia (inability to tolerate loud noises), irritability and delirium (in small children) and seizures.

In order to diagnose meningitis medical staff may perform blood tests and usually an X-ray examination of the chest. The most important test in identifying meningitis is analysis of the cerebrospinal fluid (fluid that envelops the brain and the spinal cord). In order to do this a lumbar puncture is performed. The cerebrospinal fluid sample is examined for white blood cells, red blood cells, protein content and glucose level.

Fact File: Leprosy

Leprosy is an infectious disease caused by the bacterium *Mycobacterium leprae*. It is primarily a disease of the nerves and upper respiratory tract; skin lesions are an external symptom. Left untreated, leprosy can be progressive, causing permanent damage to the skin, nerves, limbs, and eyes. Contrary to popular belief leprosy does not cause body parts to simply fall off. A long investigation by Paul Brand discovered that insensitivity meant that wounds or lesions were left untreated; this lead to tissue deterioration. The lack of pain does not trigger an immediate response as in a fully functioning body. The disease of leprosy differs from the malady described in the Bible. The biblical disease was only translated into English as leprosy.

Worldwide, 2–3 million people are disabled because of leprosy. India has the greatest number of cases, with Brazil second and Myanmar third. In 2000, 738,284 cases were identified. Although forced quarantine is unnecessary—leper colonies still remain in countries such as India, Japan, Egypt, and Vietnam.

Effective treatment for leprosy appeared in the late 1940s with the introduction of dapsone. However, leprosy bacilli resistant to dapsone gradually developed and became widespread. It was not until the introduction of multidrug therapy in the early 1980s that the disease could be diagnosed and treated successfully within the community.

Fact File: Words

WORDS TO ADD EXPRESSION AND EMPHASIS: Eheh, Heh, Hongo, Hueegh, Kah, Koh, Kumbe, Naugh, Ngheeh, Yah, Yoh.

TANZANIAN LANGUAGES: Swahili (main language), Chigogo or Gogo (one of the 150 tribal languages)

PHRASES AND SENTENCES

Ale walamuse - Good night

Ale zo wugono gwegwe? - And how did you sleep?

Ale zo wuswero wenyu nyenye - Good evening to you both

Ati Muwaha - Well Chief

Chawalamusa - Good night

Habari yako - What's your news?

Hamba hadodo - Not even a little bit

Haya! Bwana Bishopu Yakuza - Here comes the Bishop

Haya Sukuma - Hey there, push

Hodi? – May I enter?

Hodu, nyamale - That's enough, shut-up

Mbwuka – Good day, good morning

Nadabuka - I'm hungry

Nhawule? - What's up?

Njo - Come here

Yitoboce - There's a hole in it

Zo wugono? - How did you sleep?

Zo wuswero wenyu - Good evening

WORDS IN ALPHABETICAL ORDER

Bwana – Name of respect

Bwana Chisima - The well-maker

Chibedi - Disobedience

Dudus – Fleas/insects

Heva, Bwana! - Yes, sir

Jambo - Good day

Kabisa – Absolutely

Karibu – Come in

Kaya - House

Kwaheri – Goodbye

Mbisi – Hyena

Mhungo – Malaria

Muganga – Medicine man

Nzogolo – The second cock crow

Safari – A trek

Viswanu – All right

Wugali – Porridge

Yobwa – Ibis

Mbovu kabisa – Absolutely rotten

Mpishi – Cook

Mzuri – Good

Sindiciza – To see safely home

Waganga – Medicine men

Yayagwe – Oh, my mother

Fact File: Characters

Abdul – Station Porter

Anthony – One of the kitchen staff

Blandina – The Senior Nurse

Bwana – Dr White, main character/narrator

Daudi – Hospital manager/dispenser

Dr Hannah – Australian doctor

Dr Wallace – Leprosy doctor

Elisha – Carpenter

Ernest – Out patient dresser

George – Local garage man

James – Ward Manager

Kefa – The Theatre boy/dresser

Mhutila – The Water Carrier

Mika – African preacher

Nora – Roger's Fiancée

Paulo – The blind man; also leprosy patient

Robert – The second water carrier

Roger – Daudi's younger brother; assistant cook

Samson – One of the dispensing staff

Sechelela – One of the nurses

Suliman Ludha – Indian at Handari

Timoteyo (Timothy or Tim) – The African cook.

Yuditi – The Welfare Teacher

1
African Christmas

A hyena howled dismally in the darkness.

'That one was close, Bwana,' said Timoteyo, my African cook, as he handed me up a hammer.

We were completing Christmas decorations in our make-shift house in the plains of Tanganyika Territory.

'When do you think that Christmas tree will arrive, Tim?'

'It should have come before now, Bwana. I sent Roger, the drummer...'

He didn't get a chance to finish the sentence. There was a terrific bang on the door, and a loud voice called '*Hodi*' (May I come in?).

'*Karibu*' (Come in), I replied, and a grinning face appeared over the top of a great limb of thorn-bush.

'Here's your tree, Bwana. I cut it in the forest. How will you make it stand up?'

'Find a kerosene tin outside, Roger. Fill it with earth, and plant your tree in it. Then we'll have a Christmas tree just like we used to have in Australia.'

We tacked paper streamers from the top of the rough-cut doorway to the frame of the mosquito wire of the window. I took off the lid of a box, and produced an assortment of tiny candles in pastel shades, sparkling coloured balls, and tinsel. I spread them out on the top of a cabinet made from packing-cases, stained with permanganate[1].

A series of grunts ushered in Roger, with the Christmas tree. Timothy was trying to arrange some banana leaves above our one luxury, a second-hand battery wireless set. His back was towards the Christmas tree. After about six attempts, the leaves were balanced to suit him. He stepped back to view his handiwork, and one of the sharp thorns from the Christmas tree found a tender spot! Roger roared with glee!

[1] *Potassium permanganate is a chemical compound. It can be used as a disinfectant and when dissolved in water turns to a deep purple.*

'*Kah*,' said Timoteyo, as the banana leaves fell off on to the floor.

'Would you like to help decorate the tree, Roger?'

His eyes sparkled. '*Yah!* I have never seen anything like this before!'

We stuck candles on to the long thorns, and tied on intriguing parcels, wrapped in decorated paper – for Christmas – Christmas in Central Africa!

From the hills behind the village came the rumble of thunder.

'It'll rain tonight, Bwana,' said the cook, as he adjusted a huge paper ball. 'We must put everything out of range of the leaks.'

'Are you sure it will rain, Timoteyo? We haven't had a drop for eight months.'

'It always rains on Christmas Eve. It's the custom here in Ugogo. Come and look, Bwana.'

Outside it was intensely black, and the wind had dropped. Over the hills lightning flickered. There was a distant rumble of thunder, and the wonderful smell of rain on parched ground.

I had one final look at the store-room where, among kegs of Epsom salts, piles of cotton wool, and huge stock bottles of various medicines was a great pile of festively decorated bags. Into each of these, earlier in the evening, we had put a pencil, a small note-book, a cake of soap, and a great chunk of brown sugar carefully wrapped in grease-proof paper. Each was labelled with the name of a hospital patient or helper. We sorted them out carefully into big baskets in preparation for the morrow's festivities.

Timoteyo watched me adjust two overflowing stockings in the children's room. He smiled. 'All is finished now. Good night, Bwana. Sleep in peace.'

'Good night. Sleep under the shadow of the Pleiades,' said I, using a Gogo farewell.

Time grinned. 'More likely under a leak in the roof, Bwana!'

Half-an-hour later I struggled under the mosquito net, tired out. It had been a hectic day. My last waking memory was listening to the familiar strains of *Good King Wenceslas* being sung vigorously by some enthusiastic Africans as they walked along the narrow paths through the village.

In the distance came the thumpa-thumpa-thump of drums at a native dance. In the thorn bush by the river a hyena laughed. The carollers started on *The First Noel*, but I heard nothing after the second verse... I fell asleep and dreamt of home.

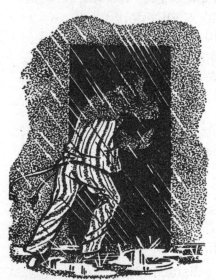

Suddenly I awoke. The whole house shook as it was struck by a terrific gust of wind. I jumped out of bed, and rushed outside to pull down the blinds and close the shutters. I was still struggling in the dark to fix the ties when the rain came pelting down. I was soaked in a second, but somehow tied the blind down, and clamped the shutters tight. I dashed through the door, a very bedraggled figure, water streaming from my pyjamas. I fumbled with a hurricane lantern, but four matches lay dead on the uneven concrete floor before I succeeded in lighting it. The rain poured down like a waterfall. I completed my preparations for the inevitable flood in the house.

Quickly I grabbed a collection of dishes, pots, tins and basins, and put them in strategic places. One I put in the middle of the only arm-chair, the second on my desk, the third on the upper octave of our dilapidated piano, and then, dashing for the children's room, moved their cots to areas of comparative dryness, and carefully covered their stockings with my wife's umbrella. Then I thought of the great pile of bulging Christmas bags, with their high sugar content, and shuddered to think of what a gallon or two of that tropical deluge would do to them. I hurried to cover them all with some rubber sheeting from the hospital store, and then went to look more leisurely at the condition of things in the house. With the aid of my torch I peered out of the window, and could see nothing but great gusts of wind-driven rain. The whole of the hillside seemed a river of brown rushing water. Above the noise of the rain beating on the tin roof, I could hear the roar of the rivers coming down from the hills. The darkness was split every second or two by vivid forked lightning, followed almost at once by a bombardment of thunder.

I visited my various dishes, emptying some, adjusting others, and then – as suddenly as it had begun – the rain ceased. The clouds blew over, and the moon shone out over the saturated country-side. The rivers on each side of us were running a 'banker'[2]. I wondered what had happened at the hospital, but was not left long in doubt, for the dresser on night-duty came to report.

'Nothing much happened, Bwana. We juggled the beds round a bit. Only one patient got really wet. He was the young man whose arm the crocodile bit. He jumped out of bed, slipped on the wet concrete, and knocked over the water bucket. How we all laughed!'

'Did he hurt his arm?'

'No, Bwana,'

'But what of the walls?'

He made a wry face. 'There are three days' work for the masons in the men's ward alone. Mud bricks will always suffer in this season.'

'How about all the decorations, Kefa?'

'There are wet streamers hanging down clammily, Bwana. They look a bit sick, but we'll put up lots of banana leaves in the morning, trust us!'

'Oh well, the roof's still on, and our wells are full. We have nothing to grumble at. And shall we not have fine crops this year?'

'Truly, Bwana, but think of the mosquitoes. Shall we not have a fine crop of them, and then much work with all the malaria this wet season?'

'Ah well, quinine's the answer to malaria. With our microscopes and syringes, pills and medicines we can fight the mosquitoes. Good night, Kefa.'

---

[2] Running a banker - an Australian term for flooding

'Good night, Bwana.'

The carollers were at it again. I could see them walking past the hospital, lighting up their way with a battered hurricane lantern.

Over the rain-soaked peanut gardens came their voices: *'Christians, Awake!'*

'Not on your life,' I smiled, as I shed my mosquito boots, and crawled into bed.

2
Cook Boy

I rescued a moth from the kerosene lamp, turned up the wick, and settled down again to check over the list of medicines that we needed at the hospital. I ticked off the item: 'Thirty thousand aspirin,' and thought to myself: 'That'll chase out a headache or two.'

A deep voice came from the door:

'*Hodi*, Bwana?'

'*Karibu*.'

In walked Timoteyo, a big stick in one hand, and a miniature hurricane lantern in the other.

'*Nhawule* (What's up), Tim?'

'Oh, it's that cook boy. His name, *Cidogowe*, means "Little Donkey," and, believe me, he's well named, Bwana. He's useless. He burned the chicken tonight. He peeled the potatoes yesterday so thoroughly that there was very little potato left, and now he's broken Bibi's best Pyrex dish. *Kah!*' He shook his head.

'Well, what do you suggest?'

'He's so clumsy, Bwana, that he would break a battleship. I wish you'd give him a permanent holiday.'

'Mmmm! But whom can you think of to take his place?'

Immediately he named his nephew, a young man who I felt would have a real talent for breaking everything within reach, including battleships.

'I'll think about it, Tim, and tomorrow...'

Anxious to show his grip of the English language, the cook interrupted: 'You-shall-give-to-him-the-bag-sir?'

'Sack, Tim, sack,' I laughed, as he closed the mosquito wire door.

'*Ale walamuse* (Good night), Bwana.'

'*Chawalamusa* (Good night), *Tim*.'

Next morning, just about eleven o'clock, I was in the out-patients' dressing-room, coat off, and sleeves rolled up.

I meant business.

'Hold his head tight, Daudi, and I'll have it out in a jiffy.'

Daudi grinned, and did his best to act as a living dental chair. I took forceps from the tray, which the nurse was holding, and grasped the offending tooth. A twist and a twirl, and I displayed the molar before the astonished eyes of the African who had had toothache for a fortnight. He had walked sixty miles to hospital to let me remove what he called his 'enemy.' He had to choose between that long journey, and letting the witchdoctor take his tooth out in little bits with a clasp-knife. He turned around to me with a big smile.

'*Yah*, Bwana, it's gone. And all in a minute!'

I watched his tongue cruising round inside his mouth. It stopped on the opposite side.

'There's one round here,' he said, 'that might give trouble. How about that?'

'All right,' I said, 'it's your tooth, but that one looks all right.'

'Oh, but it aches, and may be an enemy one day. Pull it out, Bwana.'

'As you wish,' I said. 'Hold his head, Daudi.'

I tapped the tooth gently.

'*Yaya*gwe' (Oh, my mother), howled the patient. 'It's an enemy truly.'

I picked up another pair of forceps and in a couple of minutes my patient was radiant, with the teeth wrapped in a piece of cotton wool tied in the corner of his cloth. He went outside and came back with a basket made from bark and thorn-tree twigs. In it were two very thin chickens.

'Bwana, this is my gift to you. One for each tooth.'

Solemnly I thanked him, and as he went through the door, Daudi shook with laughter.

'Oh, Bwana, did you ever see such chickens? Perhaps he thinks they will destroy your teeth. But then he doesn't know the secret of European teeth that come and go as you will.'

I laughed, and turning to him, said: 'Speaking of chickens, my cook boy has been troubling the cook mightily. He suggests young Gordon, his nephew, instead of Cidogowe, but I know what he will do to Bibi's best china.'

Daudi smiled. 'It's what the English say: A cow in the china shop, sir.'

'No, Daudi, it's a bull, not a cow.'

'But is not a bull a male cow, Bwana?'

It was getting too deep for me, so I returned to the cook boy question.

'Can you think of anybody who could do the cook boy job?'

'Well, Bwana, there's Roger, my young brother, who beats the drum. He is very punctual and very clean. He came to know Jesus after he had malaria fever in hospital.'

Daudi went off to the theatre to prepare for an operation. A minute later, James, the 'ward-manager,' walked in with an armful of sheets.

'Do you know Roger, James?'

'Oh, yes, Bwana' – putting his bundle on the table. 'I remember cutting the mud off his head when he came in.'

I shivered! James had an old cut-throat razor which he used

for shaving people's heads. He refused to allow patients to lie in hospital if they had mud in their hair because, he said, it made a mess of his pillow-cases, which were a great source of pride to him. His method of removing the mud was to grasp the edge of the red mud and tight curly hair, lift it up, and with a few adventurous sweeps of his razor, remove the whole thing. I felt sure he would scalp someone one day, but he always seemed to get away with it.

'I remember, Bwana, how one night he knelt down with me here, after I had told him about the Cross, and the living Saviour. He wanted to know just how to ask Jesus to be his Saviour, so I showed him the picture of the Light of the World and told him it was Jesus knocking at the door, and that He wanted us to open from the inside to let Him come into our hearts. I told him that verse: "If any man hear My voice, and open the door, I will come in."

'And then he said: "But isn't Jesus the Son of God? Can He not force His way through the door?"

'I told him that Jesus could, but He never did, because He wanted people to love Him, and willingly to hand their lives over to Him.'

'Did he understand it all, James?'

'He understood, Bwana. He just knelt down, and asked Jesus to take away his sin, and to help him to fight it in the future.'

'I think I'll see how he gets on for a month.'

'Good idea, Bwana! He's a decent chap, but very noisy; his laughter is like crows quarrelling. He helped me in the ward when he was getting better and should be all right. Try him for a while, anyway.'

Kefa, the theatre boy, came to the door.

'Bwana, the theatre is ready for you to sew up the man who was bitten by the hyena.'

'I'll go and patch him up now, Kefa. Call Roger. I'll talk to him after the operation.'

It was a ticklish business repairing the work of the foul teeth of a hyena, but eventually it was over, and, as I pulled off my mask and gloves some half an hour later, I was confronted by a lad of about seventeen years.

'You wanted me, Bwana?' said Roger, with a cheerful grin.

'Yes, I want a cook boy. Someone who will not break all my china, or disobey the cook, or be late for work, or half-wash the pots.'

Roger positively beamed.

'When do I start, Bwana?'

'Now,' I said. 'At the double.'

He went through the door like a rocket, jumped a small thorn-tree, and disappeared in the direction of my kitchen. Daudi was bandaging up the man's leg. He looked up and smiled.

'Roger wants to get married, and has to get twenty cows together for his dowry. He'll get them quicker now, after this rise in the world!'

3
Chickens!

They were skinning a cow under one of the baobabs near the hospital, and hacking the carcase up into pieces for sale. I noticed my cook standing among the crowd. He came over to me:

'What about some beef, Tim? It'd be a wonderful change from skinny chicken. How I have wanted to get my teeth into a piece of steak. Instead of that, I've had great difficulty in getting them out of bits of chicken!'

Tim laughed.

'I've just been standing round, Bwana, hearing the news of this cow. The man who killed it was only just one step ahead of nature. That cow's been sick for weeks, so the owner thought that he would get some profit out of it.'

'*Kah*, Tim,' I said, 'I think we will have chicken for lunch, after all.'

'I thought you would too, Bwana. But the hospital people would like some, it's all right if you cook it for a long time.'

Roger sidled up to me. 'Bwana, the hospital dressers wonder if you would buy them some meat; I could buy the cow's head and two legs for two shillings. It would cause great rejoicing, Bwana.'

'Roger,' I said, 'This cow nearly died all by itself. Would you still eat that meat? Have you the tastes of a hyena?'

'It's not as bad as that, Bwana. Anyway, who has his eyes in his stomach?'

I fished out the two necessary shillings. 'Don't blame me,' I said. 'I'll look out a bottle of castor-oil.'

But Roger was already intent on his purchase.

The cook was smiling broadly.

'You know, Tim, the veterinary officer, whom we pulled out of the mud in the river, told me a very good story about Tanganyikan chickens. He said: "There's only one way to cook them properly, so that you can both eat and digest them. They must be killed overnight, tied up in paw-paw leaves, and next day put into a large pot with four pints of water, and a pebble. You boil, and boil, and when the pebble's soft, then you know that the chicken's ready to eat."'

Timoteyo laughed.

'Kah! His mpishi (cook) must require a rest cure! When all's said and done, Bwana, chickens are best. I should know; am I not an expert? Can I not cook chickens in sixteen different ways?'

I chuckled as I thought of some of his bright ideas. He would produce what he called "Chicken Beef" by boiling the athletic bird, and soaking selected portions in Bovril. To produce chicken mutton, Timoteyo repeated the performance, but used "Bisto". Tanganyika Cutlets were made by cutting off what he termed "the bird's arms and legs," pulverising the meaty end with a chopper, and moulding the finished article with bread-crumbs. It certainly didn't taste like chicken, or anything else, for that matter, but at least it was variety!

In my early days in the country, before I was aware of the native practice of watering down milk before selling, I once met a small boy coming to my home with two bottles (long and green) and of suspicious ancestry, each of which was only half-full of milk.

'Oh,' said I, 'why are the bottles only half-full?'

The small boy spat. 'Are not the people of this town most ungenerous? I could not find one house where they would give me enough water to fill my bottles.'

On another occasion a small child arrived with a bottle full of distinctly pink milk.

"*Kah*,' I said. 'What has happened to that milk? Does it come from a red cow, or what?'

The small boy looked at me with scorn.

'Do you not know that the water is that colour everywhere these days?'

The local variety of skinny hump-backed cattle are desert born and bred. They are milked between thumb and finger. An animal in top form will produce a cupful of milk a day. The ordinary tribesman has various customs associated with the milking process which would make you a milk-hater for life.

Once when my cook's cows were dry I had to go out and purchase our milk elsewhere. Feeling sure that I was being cheated, I invested in a lactometer. The amazement of our milk-men was beyond bounds. The milk was poured into a dish. I put the nozzle of the instrument into the milk, and drew some up. Everybody standing round looked on with the greatest interest. Carefully I took a reading, squirted the milk out again, and checked my first figure. By means of an ingenious little chart supplied by the manufacturers, I could tell at a glance how much water had been put in. I shook my fist at the unfortunate milkman, who tried to hide behind one of the spectators, but they pushed him forward.

'You rogue,' I said. 'Now I know you have put water into this milk. You poured more than a cupful into each bottle.'

'*Yah*,' said the old man, 'he is better than our witchdoctors. Behold, has he not got eyes a mile long? It is useless to try and deceive him.'

The cook solemnly shook hands with the cook boy, and said:

'Is it not worth while to work in this house?'

But the boy wasn't listening. He was convulsed at the attempts of the old man to pour his rejected milk back into the narrow-necked bottles out of the large dish.

4

Mosquitoes

The lame carpenter and I were walking carefully over the roof of the men's ward.

'Solder up this hole, Elisha, and see that this sheet of iron is nailed down firmly again, and clean out the gutter at that corner.'

The African nodded.

'Are all the well-lids in order?'

'Yes, Bwana. Not a solitary mosquito will breed there this year.'

'Good. I will help you with that gutter.'

'But, Bwana, will you have time?'

'I think so.'

The carpenter smiled at me.

'Perhaps, Bwana. You have not seen what I have seen.'

He pointed with his chin beyond the water-covered mud flats to the road, a mere winding track through the corn-fields, where perhaps two miles away could be seen a procession making its way to hospital. One of the dressers had seen it, too

'Here comes trouble, Bwana.'

As they came closer I saw a native ambulance carried by two men. Then, one behind the other, walked some twenty men and women. The rear was brought up by a small boy dragging a reluctant goat by its hind leg.

I left the carpenter to his soldering, and went to greet the cavalcade.

A man came forward to greet me.

'*Mbukwa* (Good morning), Bwana.'

'*Mbukwa.*'

'*Zo wugono*?' (How did you sleep?)

'*Alezo wugono gwegwe*?' (And how did you sleep?)

'Is it well at your home?'

'All is well. And at yours?'

'And what do you eat these days?'

'Only porridge,' I replied. 'And what do you eat?'

'Only porridge,' he answered.

I wanted to know what was in that blanket tied on to a rough-cut pole carried by the two African stalwarts, but custom forbade that I should speak of that until all the greetings were over.

'What of your garden?' he asked.

'All is well,' I replied. 'And yours?'

'It is well,' he answered.

At last, after further words, he said:

'Behold, we have brought a sick one.'

34

'O-o-o-h,' I said. 'And what is his sickness?'

'He has had fever for ten days.'

'And why did you not bring him sooner?'

'Behold, was he not being treated by the medicine man?'

'Aha-a-a,' I replied. 'Was he helped?'

The man looked nervously towards his relatives and in a low voice, replied:

'We think the child is dying, so we brought him to you.'

'O-o-o-o-h. Did *Muganga,* the medicine man, send you to me?'

The African dresser by my side smiled.

The man looked uncomfortable.

'Never mind, my friend. Let us see the child, and we shall try to help him.'

Gently they lowered the pole, and undid the basket. The relatives crowded round. In front of me, on the hospital veranda, lay a small boy, eight or nine years of age, dressed only in a loin cloth. He was completely unconscious, and lay there rigid, his body burning with fever. There were livid cuts on his stomach, and small gashes underneath his chin – the work of my rival.

'Behold,' said I. 'Has he been helped by the *Muganga?*'

The relatives stood silent. The dresser picked him up and carried him into the ward. The African lad whom I had trained to use a microscope arrived with his tray of slides, needles, and stains. Grasping the child's finger firmly he pricked it and squeezed a drop of blood on the slide. Drying it, he ran off to examine it in his laboratory.

I turned to the native nurse who was making notes in the ward-book.

'Temperature 105.2°. I can hardly feel his pulse. I doubt that he can recover.'

We went out to the relatives.

'He is very, very ill. Oh that you had brought him in sooner.'

'Will he die?' asked the father, in a hushed voice.

Before I could answer, the grandmother, a thin, wild-looking woman, flashed round on him:

'Of course he will die. If our doctors could do nothing for him, what can these Europeans do, with their strange ways, and their strange medicines?'

The old African hospital matron turned to them, as they stood there in the brilliant sunshine of the tropical forenoon.

'Am I a European?' she said. 'Do I not know our customs? Do I not know that the way of our Bwana here is a better way than that of our customs, and that his medicine works where ours fail? Have you not come here because the witchdoctor is beaten?'

They stood in silence, the men leaning on their spears, the women squatting against the wall.

'Listen, my friends,' I said. 'We do not rely on medicine only. We are here because we know God. We can speak to Him, and we know that He will answer. I tell you frankly, my medicines are not enough to save this lad's life unless we have the help of God. Let us ask Him to help us now.'

The grandmother spat!

'I will have none of this,' she said, and stalked out of the hospital grounds.

'Bwana, take no notice of her,' said the father. 'Speak to God.'

Simply, and in their own language, I asked God to guide my judgment, and to spare the child's life, and to convince the relatives that God's way was the only worth-while way in this world and in the world hereafter.

I turned back to the ward, to find the African dresser ready with his report.

'He has bad malaria, sir. Very bad fever indeed. Very much of his blood is attacked by many malaria parasites.'

'Right,' I said. 'Call Daudi. I want syringes, needles, and quinine.'

'He is here, Bwana. I called him on my way over.'

The small boy had malaria of the brain – cerebral malaria. Carefully I injected quinine into a vein. I left instructions with the African nurse, and the mother was allowed to sit on a three-legged stool beside the cot. During my late afternoon round of the hospital I gave the child another injection, and had a sense of foreboding as I listened to his gasping breathing, and saw that his temperature was still 105.

The cook boy's head appeared round the door:

'Bwana, your dinner is ready.'

Nothing more could be done for the moment, so I went back to my house.

It was just after midnight when I was again called to the hospital. As I sleepily pulled on my mosquito boots my foot touched something at the bottom on one of them. I hastily pulled the long boot off, and out shot a scorpion! I dealt with it rapidly and forcibly, got into some clothes and made my way up to the hospital. A jackal yelped in the peanut gardens beyond the hospital, and through the still night air came the braying of local donkeys. It was two o'clock before I left the maternity ward. The mother and her amusing-looking twins were all well, and I thought I would just pop in to see how the little lad was. I walked into the ward, and could hardly believe my eyes. Two big feet were sticking up over the end of the cot.

It was the grandmother!

I pulled her feet, and said:

'*Eh*, what are you doing?'

A sleepy head appeared at the other end, and an irate voice replied:

'What are you disturbing me for? Have I not been insulted? Was this child not given a bed, and was not I left to sleep upon the floor?'

'Were you not told to stay at home?' I retorted, 'and not to interfere with the treatment of the child? Do not you, an old woman of the village, know the customs of the tribe? Do you wish to disobey the words of the doctor? Is it not forbidden?'

'Oh,' she said. 'Then what must I do?'

'Go,' said I, 'and go quickly!'

She shuffled out of the room, and I hastened to pick up the child. He had been pushed under the bed on to the cold concrete, and was lying there naked and gasping. His pulse was fluttering. I jumped for the injection tray, and gave him a strong stimulant. In a few moments the pulse started to fade away again. I repeated the injection. A sleepy night nurse brought two hot-water bottles. Through the dark hours of the early African morning we fought to save the little fellow's life. At five o'clock I felt that he was distinctly better, and I went home, hoping to get an hour or two's sleep. Outside I found the grandmother crouching behind a wall, trying to get back to the child. She thought she could help him, but I knew otherwise, and, taking her firmly by the hand, we went together to her house. All the way she was an unwilling listener to a vivid programme of what would happen if she entered the hospital again without my permission.

My head seemed hardly to have touched the pillow when I was called again. I groped for the hurricane lantern, and then realised that it was already dawn.

Lying gasping on the hospital veranda was a man who had been shot by an arrow. While the operating theatre was being prepared I went in to see our little patient. His temperature was down to 101, and his neck had lost some of its rigidity. I walked to the theatre, and by eleven o'clock the operation was over, and three inches of arrowhead had been removed from the man's internal mechanism. One more peep at the small boy showed him to be definitely improved. Ordering another injection, I dragged myself wearily off to bed. The next evening he opened one eye, and said:

'Bwana, *Nadabuka*,' (I'm hungry).

The happiest thing I heard for days. Two days later he was running round the hospital grounds. Then within a fortnight of his arrival, the father, the mother, the uncles, the aunts, the friends and the relatives waited upon me in deputation to ask if they might take the small boy home.

'Yes,' I said. 'You may.'

'Bwana, we see in his recovery the hand of God. We know now that these new ways are much better than our Gogo customs. We want to learn more about Jesus.'

At that moment Roger arrived with tea. 'If they give a cow as a "thank you," may I buy it, Bwana? I've still ten cows to get for my dowry.'

His brother smiled at me.

'Do you notice how eager he is to bring your tea these days, Bwana? Has not his Nora got fever, and does she not smile at him through the window of the ward?'

Roger had tactfully withdrawn out of earshot!

An hour later I sat at my front door and watched my little patient and his relatives walking home over the plains to their village. All his relations had turned to *sindiciza* him (to see him safely on his way home). They were a merry, laughing crowd; even the grandmother was smiling. The little lad ran on in front to meet his small friend who stood waiting to welcome him back to his *kaya* (his house).

'Well!' I said, to the kitchen staff. 'Did we waste two shillings in saving that life?'

The cook boy looked up from where he was splitting bits of thorn-tree with an old meat chopper.

'Is not a child worth the price of a thin sheep, Bwana?'

5

Eggs and Roger

The egg floated to the top.

'M-m-m-m-m,' said the cook.

The little boy who was selling the eggs lifted half a dozen more from the gourd in which he was carrying them. Roger put them into a large dish of water. Another one floated to the surface. The little boy grinned: 'The

hen in our house has been sitting on those eggs for a week. I wondered about them.'

'M-m-m-m-m,' said the cook. 'I don't wonder!'

I came across to watch the fun. The cook carefully counted out the small round coins with the hole in the middle in payment for the eggs that were good. The small boy, who had no pockets, tied them on a strip of cow-hide and strung them round his neck.

'Where did the chicken lay the eggs, Chikoti?' I asked.

'In our house, Bwana, underneath the grain bin, near where I sleep.'

'Where is your house?'

'Right over there,' pointing with his chin, and raising the pitch of his voice. 'Over beyond the thorn-bush jungle where the lion killed the cow last week.'

'What is it like?'

'Oh, it is built of mud, Bwana, and has a mud roof, mud walls, mud floor, and the only windows are tiny holes not big enough to put your hand through. We nearly always block these up with old bits of cloth to keep out snakes.'

'*Kah!*' I said. 'I hate snakes.'

'So do I, Bwana, and it's very frightening when you sleep on a bit of cow-skin on the floor. When I am bigger I shall have a mat of my own, and when my father's blanket wears out, he will tear it into two pieces. My big brother will get the big piece, and I will get the little bit. Then we'll cover up our heads, and sleep like grown people.'

The cook smiled at me over the little chap's head.

'In these mud houses there lives a creature worse than lions or baboons, or even man-eating crocodiles, Bwana. It's not very big, and it hides away in dark corners during the day-time, but at night it comes out and bites. We Africans call it a *dudu*. You call it a mosquito, I think, Bwana.'

'Yes, Chikoti, mosquitoes carry *mhungo* (malaria). You know, mosquitoes kill a hundred times more people than lions and leopards do.'

'Many of our tribe do not know these things, Bwana. They build great spiky thorn fences to keep away the wild animals, but never bother about the mosquitoes. If you could see an African family lying in their mud house, the grown-ups each rolled in a blanket, with their heads completely covered up and their feet sticking out – they think the mosquitoes can do less harm to that end – if you could see the little ones coiled up, kept warm only by a string of beads round their necks, and little bells round their ankles, you'd realise what a feast the mosquitoes have.'

Daudi, the dispenser, arrived at that moment.

'A roll of cotton wool, please, Bwana. We need lots for those men with the ulcers.'

I went to get it from the store. When I came back there was a great argument going on between Daudi and his young brother, who helped the cook. Daudi deftly caught the cotton wool, and pointed to Roger with his chin.

'He thinks, Bwana, that he knows more about malaria fever than I do. I, who am a hospital dresser!'

'I ought to know,' retorted his younger brother. 'I have had fever more often than you, and did I not nearly die with it? Did not the Bwana stick me very full of needles and save my life with his bitter quinine?'

'Tell me your side of the story, Roger.'

'It was after the rains, Bwana. The mosquitoes were everywhere. I got badly bitten, but felt all right for two, three, four days, and then I started to get pains – pains in my head, my neck, my chest, my back, my tummy, my legs, and all I could do was to sit miserably in the sun.

'*Huh*,' said my father, 'it's only fever.'

'I couldn't even get an aspirin to take away my headache. The sun was burning hot. I sat on a stool wrapped in a blanket, in its full blaze. Still I shivered, my teeth chattering as the fever gripped me. If you had put a thermometer into my mouth you would have found my temperature 105°. Suddenly the cold feeling started to disappear and I felt terribly hot – and – perspired – o-o-o-o-o! e-e-e-e-e-e!'

'*Kah*,' said Daudi, 'and didn't you make a fuss!'

Roger took no notice, and continued:

'I dragged myself into the darkness of the mud house again and coiled up on my cow-skin. I tried to keep cool in the stuffy atmosphere of the house.

My mother was cooking the midday meal. There is no chimney in our house, and the smoke blew down and made me cough.

'The cows are kept in the house, and they stumbled over me in the darkness. I couldn't see the goats, but my nose told me they were there. The pain in my neck became worse, and all the time I scratched and scratched, as innumerable insects walked over me. I was utterly miserable. That is what happens to us here in Africa, when we have got no medical missionary to help. I lay there for two days, Bwana, and then everything went black.'

'*Huh*,' said Daudi, his brother, 'black for you, and black for me! I had to help to carry you to the hospital in a blanket, and you were heavy!'

'*Huh*, and black for me,' said I. 'I remember. I was asleep in my house, dreaming I was eating ice-cream, a thing I hadn't seen or tasted for years, when suddenly I heard voices:

'"*Hodi*, Bwana, *hodi?* Wake up, wake up!"'

'I sat up in bed.

'What's up?'

'"A sick one has been carried to hospital. He has just arrived. He is very sick, very sick."'

'I made my way to the hospital along the path between the baobab trees. As I walked, I yawned. Suddenly I was wide awake. I knew something was following me. I could feel my hair stand on end. I swung the lantern round, and, not ten yards behind me were the white fangs of a creature about the size of an Alsatian dog, slinking along towards me. I grabbed my stick, and moved towards it. It let out a sudden howl, and I jumped a foot in the air. But the howl told me that it was only a hyena, and hyenas will not hurt you unless you fall down, and I certainly was not going to fall down!

'And then I found that you were my patient, Roger, but you were different then. You had mud in your hair and charms on your arms.'

'Yes, Bwana. Those were the days before I knew about Jesus Christ; before I had given my life to Him, before I even knew I needed a Saviour.'

'Anyhow, we got him off to bed, didn't we, Daudi, and examined his blood under the microscope.'

'Bwana, I have often wanted to ask. What did you see down the spout of the microscope?'

'We saw things, Roger, like pink peach petals. They were blood cells. There were also tiny little things that looked like purple signet rings. These showed that you had bad malaria.'

'Bwana,' said Daudi, 'did we not give him many injections, and did not he swallow many pills?'

'Ugh,' said Roger. 'But I was terribly glad when my neck lost its stiffness.'

'Do you think, Bwana, he was worth the ten shillings we spent saving his life?'

Hastily he dodged a bit of firewood that his younger brother tossed at him.

6
Eyes

'I refuse! I refuse! *Yayagwe* (Oh, my mother). I don't want to go. *Yayagwe*.'

The tall African took no notice of the struggles of the small boy whom he was dragging along by one hand or the bleating of the rather skinny goat he was pulling along with the other. The small boy kept up a continuous wail.

'*Hodu, nyamale*' (That's enough; shut up), snapped his father.

The small boy looked up helplessly. His eyes were red and swollen, and flies crawled unheeded over his tear-stained face.

'My father, I do not wish to go to the witchdoctor; did not his medicine ruin the eyes of my friends, Mazengo and Mabawa?'

Frantically the little lad tried to get away, but he was held tightly.

The father strode on over the desert road across mile after mile of arid country. Walking through matted thorn-bush, they came to a village where the mud huts were clustered together under a group of baobabs. Stopping before the largest of these, the father, after going through elaborate greetings, told his tale to the witchdoctor. The latter, dressed in a dirty cloth knotted over one shoulder, was sitting on a three-legged stool under a great thorn-tree. Around his arms were strips of cow-hide with charms in them. His earlobes were stretched, and reached half-way down to his shoulders. You could easily have put your closed fist through the hole. In them were a mass of brass and iron ornaments. He was much more interested in the goat than in his patient. When he was satisfied that the animal was fat enough he grunted and went into the house. Returning with an axe, he stalked off into the forest. He paused, glanced furtively around and then chipped some bark from a tree, cut it into shreds, and chewed it up. Walking still farther, he climbed among the rocks on a strange little hill, and made a jagged gash in a cactus, catching the sap as it ran out. Scooping some of this up with his filthy hands, he added it to the collection he was chewing. Finally he sought out a tree with pennant-shaped leaves. He pulled three, rubbed them in his hands, put the pulped mess into his mouth, and masticated it with all the other stuff, his jaws moving like those of a cow.

'Bwana,' said Daudi, who was telling me this story, 'you know what witchdoctors' mouths are like! Do you remember when you pulled out old Lengholo's teeth, how you wore a mask, and the thickest gloves you could find?'

'Ugh...' I shuddered. 'I well remember it!'

'*Hodi*,' said a voice at the door.

'*Karibu*,' said Daudi.

It was Roger, stuttering with excitement and pain.

'I thought a pot was empty, but it was half-full of boiling water, and I spilt it on my foot!'

Daudi poured some picric acid into a bowl, and painted the burnt area. He threw Roger a bandage.

'Bandage it up yourself,' he said. 'You're the Bwana's cook boy. You ought to know how to do it by now.'

He came to the door, and pointed down the road with his chin.

'*Kah!* Bwana. Look!'

Coming towards us was a young man being led by a small boy. As they came level I saw the man was stone blind.

'*Mbukwa*, Paulo,' said Daudi.

'*Mbukwa*, Daudi,' came the reply.

'*Zo wugono*?' (How did you sleep?)

'*Ale zo wugono*.'

'I've just been telling the Bwana your story, Paulo. I've got to the place where the witchdoctor had been to the forest and collected his bark and things and was chewing them up in his mouth.'

The blind man groped his way towards a seat and then took up the tale himself.

'Will I ever forget it? Was it not the last thing I ever saw before this great darkness came upon me?' He paused.

'I can still see that old man with his axe over his shoulder, his mouth bulging, walking back to where I

sat cowering. He sat down on the stool again, grabbed my head firmly, holding it between his knees. Dragging my eyelids apart, he spat the contents of his mouth into my eyes. I twisted my head and bit him. He lost his balance and fell over backwards. I ran for my life back along the path. I have never experienced such pain as during those hours of running through the bush. At first I could see in a blur; then I saw light only.

I stumbled and fell. Since then I've lived in darkness. My eyes were ruined! Ruined for life!'

His hand strayed to the dressing-room table, and he picked up a bottle with an eye-dropper in it.

'And to think, Bwana, that even this small bottle of eye medicine … how much would it cost?'

'Oh, about threepence,' I replied.

'To think that this bottle would have saved my eyesight!'

He sighed. 'I have to be led by the hand, and am blind – blind!'

He put his head in his hands, and sat dejectedly, toying with the bottle of eye-drops which, while they would help others, could never help his own eyes.

I turned to Roger.

'Take Paulo down to your kitchen and give him tea, and bring him back later.'

'*Heva*, Bwana!' (Yes, sir).

As I turned back to the hospital, the out-patient dresser came to me, and said:

'Bwana, there are four cases waiting in the eye-room.'

'What are they, Ernest?'

'Two eye ulcers, a man whose eyes are utterly ruined, also a little boy whose eyes are very swollen – he is terribly frightened.'

I walked into the dressing-room. Huddled in a corner was a little chap of perhaps eight years. He was moaning. 'Oh, my mother! Oh, my mother! Don't let him touch me.'

I sat down at my desk and said:

'What's the matter, old fellow?'

He turned to me with surprise.

'You, a European, speak our language?'

'Yes,' I said. 'I speak your language, and I want to help you. What's the trouble?'

'I don't want medicine. It hurts!'

I smiled. 'Look at this.'

In a frightened way, he looked at the bottle of eye-drops which I held in my hand.

'This medicine will make your eyes better in five days. You will be able to play with your companions again, and there will be no more pain.'

'Oh, *ya*, *ya!*' he cried. 'Are not all *Waganga* (medicine men) liars?'

Everybody in the dressing-room laughed.

'Well,' said I, 'to show you that this medicine does not hurt, I will put it into my own eyes.'

'*Kah*,' said everybody. 'Who ever heard of a medicine man using his own medicine on himself?'

'Bwana,' said the little boy. 'If they put medicine into your eyes, and you don't cry, then medicine can be put into my eyes.'

Again everybody laughed.

I turned to the dresser: 'Ernest, put drops into my eyes.'

I sat next to the small boy on a wooden form. The dresser, armed with an eye-dropper and some cotton wool, pushed back my eye-lid, and put two drops into each of my eyes.

'Does it hurt you, Bwana? Does it sting?'

'Not yet,' I replied.

'Ya ... I will wait for a few minutes and see what happens.'

'All right,' I said, and went over and wrote his name in the eye-patient book. The dresser turned to the waiting people.

'With this medicine we saved the eye-sight of three hundred children last dry season.'

The little boy moved across to where I was sitting. He put his hand in mine, and said:

'I am ready now, Bwana. I trust you, but I want you to put the drops in.'

I cleaned his eye with lotion, put in the drops, and he shut his eyes tight.

'*Ya*, truly, it hurts no more than the water in the salty well.'

There was a pause as he blinked, then:

'Bwana, can I have one of those green eye-shades? The glare of the sun makes my eyes so sore.'

'Right-oh, old chap. Here you are. Come again this afternoon, and tomorrow, and five more days.'

He smiled up at me. 'I'll come!'

As I wrote his treatment down in the record book I could not help thinking of twenty little people that I had seen in a village only four hours' walk from the hospital, who were stone blind. Empty sockets told a tragic story of the witchdoctor's treatment. A pound's worth of eye-drops would have saved every eye. A doctor in Tanganyika can do amazing things in saving suffering at an absurdly small cost in money.

The dresser had my first patient ready for a minor operation.

I scrubbed up my hands and put on my gown. Drops had been put into the man's eyes, to take away the pain. My assistant stood beside me, holding a tray on which were a dish containing sharpened match-sticks and three small bottles. I put a drop from one of these into the patient's eye. Immediately a bright green patch showed up in the very centre. There was an ulcer eating into the actual substance of the eye.

'Keep very still, my friend,' I said. 'Do not move even a little bit. There will be no pain.'

'Yes, Bwana,' he breathed through clenched teeth.

I took up a match-stick, dipped it in pure carbolic, and carefully moved it right over the surface of the ulcer, taking the greatest care to touch every bit of that ugly green mass. It was a ticklish business. Push the match one-sixteenth of an inch too far, and one could easily ruin the eye. Push it not far enough, and the treatment would not be effective. I satisfied myself that all was in order. Black drops were put into the eye, and my assistant gently placed a pad and bandage in position, and handed the patient twelve aspirin, which he tied in the corner of his cloth.

'Listen,' said the African dresser. 'Take two of those pills at sunrise, midday, and sunset. Do not follow the path of the ignorant, and swallow them all at once, like the local water-carrier. He drank the whole bottle of medicine at one go, to get better quickly, and nearly poisoned himself.'

Everybody roared with laughter.

'How did you get your ulcer?' I said, as I prepared to deal with the second man.

'Oh, Bwana, I was walking through the forest in the dark, beyond the third river where the thorn-trees are very thick, and I heard a hyena behind me. So I ran, and a thorn from an over-hanging branch went right through my eyelid into my eye. My brother treated it by licking my eye.'

'*Kah…*' said the dresser. 'No wonder you have developed an ulcer!'

'But,' said the man, 'how did I know it was the wrong thing to do? Is it not our custom? Have we not all lived in fear of eye-sickness until the hospital came?'

The saddest job that morning was telling the blind man who had been led by the hand for fifty miles that I could do nothing for him. His eyes were ruined, utterly ruined, by native medicine.

'Can you do nothing, Bwana? Can you not try your medicines? You cannot understand what it feels like to live in darkness. Won't you try?'

The head dresser came into the room.

'Listen,' he said. 'If a man has his arm cut off, can he grow another?'

'No,' said the blind man. 'He cannot.'

'And if he has his eyes spoiled, can he grow new eyes?'

'No,' said the man. 'I suppose he can't.'

Paulo had returned just in time to hear our talk. He groped his way over to the blind man, and sat next to him.

'I am blind too. I suffer as you suffer. It is always night to me, as it is to you.'

The blind patient shook his head. He was numb with sorrow.

'I had hoped for so much. For three days I have walked and walked – hoping – always hoping, but even the Bwana can do nothing.'

His voice trailed away.

Paulo had his arm round the other blind man's shoulder and was gently explaining that there was still light for one's soul.

7
Unfenced Zoo

'Good morning, Doctor,' said the black-bearded Sikh conductor. 'Are you visiting your hospitals?'

'Yes, I'm going to Saranda Station, and then to Kilimatinde Hospital. What's up with the old train today, conductor? She's slower than ever.'

'I regretfully would like to inform you, sir,' said the tall Indian, 'that this is due to the dampness of the wood which is the fuel of the locomotive. However, we shall only be three hours late.'

This was nothing unusual, and I sighed contentedly as I thought: 'At any rate, I'll be at the hospital in time for dinner.'

The Tanganyika Express wound its way slowly over the plains. Some blue and white spotted guinea-fowl that had been feeding near the line flew off clucking into the thorn-bush. Half a dozen big baboons, chattering and scratching, swung their way through the undergrowth. It was breathlessly hot. The train went even slower, and laboured its way up a steep slope. We were climbing the great Rift Wall. Round and round we dragged, at almost walking speed. A big African, herding some thin, humped-back cattle, leant on his stick, and watched us.

At long last we pulled up at a station. The African station-master walked about, waving a variety of flags. The conductor ordered the porters around, and I handed my bag through the window to a tall Arab with a fez at a rakish angle. I greeted him in Kiswahili.

'*Jambo* (Good day), Abdul. *Habari yako* (What's your news)?'

'*Mzuri* (Good), Bwana.'

'Abdul, can you run me over to the hospital at Kilimatinde? I've got my cook boy with me.'

'Yes, Bwana, I'm going there, and shall take you both if you will travel in my lorry.'

I handed my ticket to the African station-master, who said, with a rich Scottish accent: 'Thank ye, sir,' and turning to the conductor: 'Wait a moment now, and I'll gie ye a hand wi' that parcel.'

He was a Nyasalander[1], and had been educated there by a Scottish Presbyterian Mission.

---

[1] Nyasaland became Malawi in 1964. It was called the Central Africa Federation in colonial times.

Behind the white-washed station buildings stood a mechanical patriarch. I stood and looked at it, and laughed. What a machine!

I climbed into it. Both its mudguards had fallen off ages ago, and the windscreen had been broken two years before that; if I could believe the smiling, coal-black lad who was filling the radiator from a rusty kerosene tin!

Abdul loaded some tins of petrol, a roll or two of calico, two bags of peanuts, and a bale of cotton blankets, on to the back. Roger arranged himself amongst this baggage, and with a grind and a grunt we were off along the narrow straight road cut through almost impenetrable jungle. Masses of thorn-trees grew right up the side of the track. Geese and other birds, screaming raucously, flew among the taller trees that appeared above the tangle of thorns. Here and there were tracks where an elephant had crashed its way through the undergrowth. Occasionally we came to a deep and narrow water-course.

It was a wild spot.

'I have brought my rifle, Bwana. This road is always full of animals, and you never know what's just over the next hill.'

'Did I not have to walk along this road on my last Safari up here? Your machine had a broken axle. It was late in the afternoon, and when we passed that thick bit of jungle over the next hill, I felt I would come face to face with something, and sure enough I did. An animal roared in the undergrowth. I stopped – there was a rustling of branches, and out rushed a wart-hog and a litter of six little pigs. They looked at me, grunted, and disappeared into the jungle the way they had come.'

Abdul laughed. We were just coming to the crest of a little hill. But his laugh died on his throat as we came over the rise.

'O-o-o-o-o,' said Roger's voice behind me.

Abdul's hand flew to the brake. I could feel something in my throat and wanted to swallow, but was unable. For there – coming towards us, right down the centre of the road, was a fearsome-looking, black-maned lion!

Abdul groped for the rifle.

'*Yah*,' said Roger's frightened voice behind me. 'Behold, my blood has turned to water.'

Abdul squinted down the sights of his rifle. He could choose the eye shot, which is both difficult and dangerous, or wait to shoot him through the heart. For this the lion must oblige and turn slightly to the left.

He came on – and on – slowly but steadily – ever closer to us. I pressed my feet against the footboard of the car, and did not feel encouraged when I noticed the way Abdul's hand shook as he held the rifle. The Africans at the back sat huddled behind the baggage. Suddenly the lion stopped and turned, giving the Arab just the opportunity he wanted. He pressed the trigger. The report still re-echoed through the forest as the lion turned his head towards us – and came on. Abdul made furious efforts to eject the spent cartridge, but it was stuck – and then I noticed the lion's legs shake, and when he was not fifteen yards away, he collapsed.

'Phew,' said Abdul, 'I didn't like that!'

In the meantime Roger's water had turned back to blood, and I had swallowed the what-not in my throat. Full of resolution we got out of the dilapidated lorry, and went to look at the creature. A small African boy pulled it by the tail. We stood round the carcase, estimating its size and weight, when I noticed Roger staring over my shoulder in a fixed way.

'What's the matter?' I asked.

'Ugh… Look…'

Emerging from the forest farther down the road was the lion's mate. A huge lioness! Hastily we got back into the lorry!

'I couldn't shoot two in the one day,' said the Arab, as he put the lorry into gear, 'I'm sure I couldn't.' I have seldom travelled farther or faster in reverse! When we stopped, we talked of everything but lions for twenty minutes, and then made careful reconnaissance over the top of the rise. At last, when we saw that the coast was clear, we drove on to the C.M.S. Hospital. I was full of the story of our journey, but did not have the chance to tell it. I was met outside the ruins of an old German fort by the Australian nurse in charge.

'Oh, Doctor, I'm so glad you've arrived. You're just in time. A little boy has been carried in from forty miles away with an arrow wound in his eye.'

I had just time to gulp down a cup of tea before going into the operating theatre. It was a very ticklish business that operation, but half an hour later, the little chap was lying in a cot covered with a patch-work quilt made by friends in Australia. I felt we had every chance of saving his eye. I shuddered when I thought what might have happened if we had not won the confidence of the family before. The witchdoctor could be relied upon to produce some atrocity in such an emergency.

I felt a touch on my arm.

'Doctor,' said the African nurse. 'Would you come and have a look at the dressing of a small boy? His head was bitten by a hyena. We sewed it up and put antiseptic medicine on it. It looked as though he had been scalped when he arrived a fortnight ago, but it seems better now. You should have seen it earlier.'

She shuddered – and it takes a lot to make an African shudder.

Sitting up in his cot was a cheerful-looking little person, his head swathed in bandages.

'Hello,' I said, 'so you're the hyena's breakfast, are you?'

He laughed. 'I nearly was, Bwana. But my father heard me yelling and jumped up and beat the *mbisi* (hyena) with a stick that he pulled out of the fire.'

The nurse unwound the bandages, and I looked at the ugly wound across the back of his head. His mother stood up from the little three-legged stool on which she was sitting.

'Bwana, I thought he would have died.'

'That's more than likely,' I replied, 'if the Sister had not done the right thing, and done it quickly.'

'It is the goodness of God,' she said.

'Truly,' I replied. 'Let us just thank Him.'

So we knelt around the cot, and simply thanked God for helping us to save the little boy's life, and asked that he might use it in a useful way for Him later on. The relatives presented me with a wiry-looking chicken, which I accepted with due ceremony. As I walked down to the house with it under my arm, I told the Australian nurse about the lions.

'What a country,' she said. 'You never know what's going to happen next, do you?'

'Indeed you don't,' I said, and indeed we did not, for when we came to the house we found that it had been invaded by black ants, and had to wait five hours before we could get into the dining-room! That is Tanganyika for you!

But my animal experiences were not nearly over. A week later I was back at the base hospital a hundred miles away. It was early Sunday morning. The drums were being beaten for church. I was looking forward to a quiet day. It had been a hectic week of travel, punctures, bush operations, getting stuck in rivers, and camping out in the jungle. My cook, always an optimist, had made me a jelly!

'How are you going to make that thing set, Tim,' I said.

'I'm always hoping, Bwana, that one day you will not have to drink it,' he said. 'Perhaps it will be cool today.'

'Have you ever known it to be cool here, Tim?'

'No, Bwana, but then I've only lived here thirty years!'

I fanned myself with a topee[1].

---

[1] A lightweight hat worn in tropical countries to protect you from the sun.

'*Yah!* I'm glad it's Sunday. Only very sick people will come to hospital today.'

I had hardly said this when I saw a cavalcade moving towards the hospital. I groaned, and walked out in the blazing sun to find out what it was all about.

A dresser came running to meet me down the path.

'Crocodile bites,' he panted. 'I've got the instruments on in the theatre. It's very, very bad.'

In the ward I found a girl of about ten years of age, with staring eyes, and drawn face. She was near the point of collapse. Her leg had been mercilessly bitten by one of the huge reptiles. It lay there a pulped mass. Rapidly I gave her an injection to ease her pain, and set out to treat her shock. The father came with me as I went to the theatre, to see that all was ready for the immediate operation that had to be undertaken.

'Tell me the story, father. How did it happen?' I threaded needles and picked out reels of catgut from the jars on the packing-case cupboards. Standing silhouetted against the window was the tall African, a giant of a man with a black cloth thrown over one shoulder. He started his story:

'My daughter was with the women. She was drawing water in her clay pot, Bwana, down beside the Ruaha River. It was yesterday in the afternoon. As she leant over to fill the pot, the crocodile came out of the water. She tried to get away, but slipped in the soft mud, and in a minute it had got her.'

'But how did she get away at all?' I asked.

'Oh, Bwana, she is a girl of courage. She broke her clay pot over its ugly snout. It let go, and she struggled somehow up the bank. We came quickly and drove it back into the river with spears and sticks. We did not know what to do. The river is sixty miles from here.'

'You didn't carry her all the way?' I said.

'Oh, no, Bwana. We waited beside the road till midnight. It was bitterly cold down there by the river, and she cried and cried, until she had no more tears. Then an Indian lorry picked us up, and brought us to the turn-off, ten miles from here. Oh, that journey! How we bumped and bumped!' (I thought of that nightmare stretch of road with its deep ruts and the extreme discomfort I had touring it in a car.)

'We tried to make her comfortable on the floor of the lorry. But it was terribly hard, and she groaned and groaned. Since dawn I have been carrying her on my back through the swamps to here. Can you do anything for her, Bwana?'

'We'll try,' I said, but at that minute I heard Daudi turn out the primus.

'The things aren't ready yet, are they Daudi?'

In English he replied: 'There will be no need for the instruments today, Bwana. I've just heard that she has passed on.'

Quietly I took the father aside. 'She has gone.'

The big African put his head in his hands and simply shook in silent grief. Daudi came in and spoke quietly to him in an effort to comfort.

'Oh, my daughter, my daughter. If I could have got here sooner! It was such a journey!'

I watched the African dresser kneel beside the operating table with this great, half-clad African; silently I joined them, and Daudi committed into God's hands the soul of the little girl, and told Him about the grief of the parents. Daudi understood so fully these primitive people's feelings in tragedies of this sort. Very simply he spoke to the mourning relatives of God and of the life that is after death, and of the Saviour who makes that life possible.

I went away from the hospital with the European nurse.

'What a tragedy, Sister. What a tremendous effort they made. How futile it seems over here to attempt to combat all those illnesses, all these tropical things, these animal attacks, and the primitive transport – and to have to do it all with so few drugs and supplies. I feel utterly depressed about it all.'

'It's the hectic week you've had, Doctor, and this on top of it, that makes you look only at the dark side of the picture. Don't forget all the eyes we saved last week, and those four children with tick fever, and the baby with pneumonia, and the woman with twins in the maternity ward.'

'Oh, yes, Sister, I realise all that, but things are so difficult out here. It's a colossal task for just a handful of us to tackle.'

'Well, frankly, Doctor, we couldn't tackle it if we were not sure that God stands behind us, and helps us in every phase of the job.'

'That's exactly it, Sister.'

8
Water Carriers

'*Yitoboce!*' (There's a hole in it) said Mhutila, the cross-eyed, buck-toothed water carrier, appearing at my office door. 'When we poured water into it, behold, it squirted out through the hole, and continues to squirt out.'

He was a picturesque person with his closely-shaved head, and tattered shorts. The muscles of his arms and bare chest rippled. He was enormously strong.

I grabbed my topee, and ran with him to the place where there was a big cement drum which served as our hospital water storage tank.

'Oh, one of little wisdom,' I said. 'Why did you not put your finger over the hole, to save the water from running away?'

'What could I do, Bwana? Could I stand here all day, with my finger over the hole, while you sat writing, writing, in your little office?'

There was a definite twinkle in the eye that focused. The other blinked gloomily.

'Well now, my son. Put your finger, over that hole, and wait.'

I returned in a moment or two with a cork. The water-carrier's eye still twinkled. His finger religiously covered the hole, but the drum was empty.

'I forgot to tell you, Bwana, there was another hole on the other side!'

I looked at him hopelessly. I could get along reasonably well in three languages, but they all seemed inadequate to deal effectively with this situation!

At that moment a nurse from the babies' ward came up, jug in hand. She looked into the drum.

'No water, Bwana! What can I do? How can I bath the babies? You cannot bath them with air. You're the doctor! Please do something.'

'*Viswanu*' (All right), I said.

Then, along came a nurse from the women's ward, with a bowl in her hand. She came to the drum and, finding it dry, said to me:

'Bwana, the women won't take their medicine unless we mix it with lots of water, and there's none left in the barrel. You're the doctor, won't you...'

'*Viswanu*,' I said.

The cook was the next to appear.

'Bwana, you're a man. You don't understand about cooking, but how can we make porridge if there's no water? You're our doctor. Won't you do something about it?'

I looked to Mhutila for support, but he had slipped off already to the well, a mile and a half away, his two buckets swinging on each end of his palm-leaf carrying stick. Then, at that moment the situation was solved. I heard a high-pitched voice half singing, half chanting: 'Ci-ci-ci-ci-ci... Ya-ya-ya-ya-ya,' and finally, 'He-e-e-e-e,' and round the corner of the building came a smiling face, streaming with perspiration. It was Robert, the second water-carrier. The cook whisked away one of his kerosene tins, and the two nurses filled the jug and bowl from the other, first lifting out carefully the dried pumpkin shell that prevents the water from splashing as the water-carrier comes up the hill from the sandy river-bed.

'You were far behind your companion, Robert.'

'Yes, Bwana. This was my enemy.'

For my inspection he produced a long thorn from his tightly-curled hair!

'It went right through my foot. I stopped for Daudi to put iodine on it. *Yah*, that medicine bites!'

I carefully plugged up the holes in the drum with corks, and touched up the concrete side. That problem was solved, at any rate, for a day or two.

A few days later a large and very dusty Englishman arrived at the house. He was driving in one of those antiquated lorries that are the vogue in Tanganyika.

'Hello, Doc,' he said. 'How's the tea-pot?'

'In good form,' I replied. 'Come in and reduce your drought. What have you been doing these days, with all that clatter-trap in the back of your Juggernaut?'

'I am superintending the sinking of wells all over the country. I have to put one up – or rather, down, a few miles from here, and thought of camping over there amongst the baobabs at Makangwa.'

'How do you put these wells down?'

'Oh, we have two large iron containers. One fits inside the other. There's about three inches between the inner one and the outer one. You pour concrete into that space, and cram it down with posts, and then pour more in, and ram that down, and in that way you have the walls of your well.'

'That's a grand idea. I wish we had a couple here. These cement drums that we use for storage tanks rust in no time, and then everybody is chasing me for water for cooking or mixing medicines, or the hundred-and-one things for which water is needed in hospital.'

'Tell you what, Doc. Why not put one of these concrete tanks on the veranda of your ward? It has a concrete floor!'

'Yes.'

'And then you could use that for your storage, and there's no fear of it leaking. I'll bring over the necessary equipment on Saturday and put it up for you. I'll want ten men. Get some cracked stones as big as walnuts and about a ton of sand.'

'Thanks very much. I'll have everything ready,' I said. 'How about another cup of tea?'

Next morning there was a stream of men carrying sand in big dishes on their heads. Others were seated cracking granite to the appropriate size.

Saturday morning arrived, and with it an urgent operation. A child had been knocked about by a buffalo. I stitched him up here and there, put his arm in plaster-of-Paris where it was broken, saw him safely back into the ward, and then went to see how the well was progressing. The whole veranda was a hive of industry. My big friend had everything under way. Africans were standing on petrol boxes pounding away at the concrete which others had mixed and poured in between the iron rims. Everybody was singing, cheerful, and extremely hot.

'*Yah*,' said Mhutila, the water-carrier, resting on his pole. 'Our troubles are now ended!'

A nurse looked through the ward window and smiled. But somehow I had a lingering foreboding that all was not well.

By eleven o'clock it was finished.

'Pour some water into it,' said my big friend. 'Leave it in position, and on Monday I will come to pull off the iron rims.'

'Thanks very much,' I said. 'How about coming and having dinner with us today? The usual poultry lunch – a threepenny chicken steamed and then baked.'

We both laughed. 'And spinach?' he asked.

'And spinach,' I replied. 'Wonderful variety we have in our diet over here.'

It was Monday morning, and I was trying to listen to the chest of a small African boy, who I thought had early pneumonia. There was a terrible din outside, and I couldn't hear a thing.

'What's all the racket about, Kefa?' said I, to an African dresser who was passing the window, and grinning hugely – 'The Bwana Chisima (the well-maker) has built the well on our veranda, and now, behold he cannot get his iron things off, because the roof stops him.'

He collapsed in merriment. 'And now, behold, he is taking off your roof, so that he may have his iron rims to build other wells in other places.'

My English friend appeared at the window. 'Sorry about this old chap! We shall have to pull off a part of your veranda roof, or you will have my tank-building apparatus on your hands for life!'

I groaned as I pulled the stethoscope out of my ears.

'I felt there'd be something wrong. We couldn't have a new well here without there being some catch in it.'

My pessimism was not justified. The roof was duly restored, and the tank was the pride of our eyes. We had to secure it a little here and there with cement, but before long it was the joy of the water-carriers' hearts. Water had to be dipped out of it, however, as there is less waste this way than by using taps. Taps are not fully understood by visitors to the hospital, who turn them on, but somehow cannot bring themselves to the point of turning them off, which is not a good thing. In a few days' time, I found a long piece of hooked wire beside the well. I called Daudi to have a look at it.

'What's the wire for? Fishing?'

'Yes, Bwana,' he replied. 'Fishing for cups and jugs.' He stood back admiringly. 'There isn't another well like that in all Ugogo! Isn't it a beauty! Have you ever been thirsty, Bwana?'

'Oh, yes,' I said. 'I'm always thirsty.'

'But I mean truly thirsty. Has your tongue ever swollen? Have you got to the stage where you cannot talk?'

'No,' I said, 'I haven't.'

Daudi grinned.

'Many people have in Ugogo,' he replied. 'What's the good of money or cattle then? They'd give a hat full of money for a gourd of water. Once I dug six feet down in a sandy river bed. I dug, and dug, and when the water oozed up, I gulped it greedily, but it was salty, and I had to walk for hours before I found more. Truly, Bwana, water is our greatest need.'

The welfare teacher came along with a jug.

'Isn't it a lovely well?' she said. 'All the visitors come to look at it. They'd rather look at it than at an aeroplane.'

'Well,' said Daudi, 'you can't drink an aeroplane, can you?' Yuditi laughed.

'What people do want is something that is useful to them. That's why I'm teaching them to bath their babies with a pint of water. The Welfare Book says: "Bath baby in two gallons of warm water." That's all right in Australia, but here in Africa, where you must walk miles and miles to the well, it's a different matter.'

'Mmmmm,' I said.

'If your wife had to carry your water supply five miles on her head in a kerosene tin, she wouldn't feel like having big baths, nor bathing the baby with lots of water, would she?'

'She would not,' I replied.

'So I teach the women here how to bath baby without soap and just a pumpkin shell full of water.'

'Tell me, Yuditi, how do you do it?'

'The blue soap we can buy for fifty cakes a shilling at the hospital store is all very well, but some people won't buy. So I teach them to take wood ashes, white ones, wet them, and rub them on the baby.'

'*Kah*,' interrupted Daudi. 'That's just what we do in the Pathology Room when we clean slides with stuff called 'Bon Ami'.'

'Then,' said Yuditi, 'we rinse the baby with a little water, get off all the ashes and dirt we can, and give him a second rinse. Then you hold him out in the sun to dry. You finish up by rubbing him with peanut oil. Anyone can crush some peanuts, they grow in every garden. It may sound crude, Bwana, but it saves hundreds of children from getting skin disease, and any woman can do it. Even if she cannot afford to buy soap, she has plenty of wood ash, and nobody grudges a pumpkin shell full of water.'

'It's a grand idea,' I said. 'How's your fathercraft idea getting on? Has your husband been teaching the fathers to make cots and things?'

'Yes, Bwana, he has shown them how to make cots from creepers and the trees that grow near here. The most expensive one so far cost threepence!'

Daudi and I both laughed.

'We put the legs of the cots in jam tins, or tiny clay pots, and then the *dudus* (insects) can't crawl up the legs and bite baby. There will be no tick fever amongst the children of our village soon, when everybody has cots for the children instead of letting them lie naked on the floor on a piece of cow-skin. But, Bwana, it's only an African who can teach an African these things. It takes a European very many years to see things through our eyes, and to think as we think.'

'Quite so,' I said. 'That's why we train you to help the people of your own tribe.'

'Truly, sir,' said Daudi. 'This is the better way. Do you remember you spoke, the other morning, about receiving Jesus into our lives?'

'It was this verse, wasn't it, Daudi: "John 1:12: But as many as received Him, to them gave He power to become the sons of God, even to them that believe on His Name."'

'That's it, Bwana. But many people did not quite understand you. You put European thoughts into our African language. This is how we Africans would explain it.'

Yuditi put down her jug, and we listened to the simple story. It shows very clearly how Africans think.

'A man was travelling through the jungle,' said Daudi, 'and as he walked over the dry, dusty hills, he got more and more thirsty. At last he came to a house.

'"Water," he said, "give me water." So the man of the house brought him out a pumpkin shell full.

'"Thank you," said the man. "I am so thirsty, I need water so badly. My tongue is swollen, I am dreadfully thirsty."

'"Well, drink it," said the man who owned the house.

'"*Kah*, I am thirsty. How I need water."

'"There's your water. It's there, drink it... look... there... See... that's water. It'll quench your thirst. Pick it up in your hands man, and drink it."'

'"*Yah,*" said the man. "I see." He sat in the shade, and looked at the water, and the man of the house went out to look after his cattle. Just before he went, he said: "Pick up the dish, and drink, man. I can bring it to you, but I cannot drink it for you. It's your work to receive it, and to drink it, if you'd lose your thirst and save your life."

'But the traveller wouldn't receive the water, and he sat there till he died of thirst, with water within his reach. He knew it was water; he knew it would quench his thirst; but he didn't take it up and drink it. That's just like the people who won't receive Jesus, the Water of Life, as the Saviour from sin, and the Chief of their lives.'

'Truly, Daudi. I'm beginning to see light.'

'Your talking's got to be so simple, Bwana, that everyone can understand. That's why our hospital is very useful. We can preach by our medicines, and our operations, and make parables that even the bush people can understand.'

I nodded, and thoughtfully walked home. I looked up at the wonderful sunset. Silhouetted against the purple sky were the water-carriers on their last – the fourteenth – safari of the day.

9
Car Travel

'*Mbovu kabisa*,' said the driver most emphatically.

I turned to Roger. 'What does he say?' I asked. The lad laughed. 'He says the car is rotten – absolutely!'

I looked at the old safari-bodied car, dating back to 1929, with its broken three-ply sides and the pathetic air of shabby respectability of its patched canvas roof and polished radiator.

The driver went off again in a vitriolic burst of Swahili. My interpreter turned to me with a wide grin.

'He says, Bwana, that the car is like an old cow, it eats much and gives nothing in return but trouble.' And he burst into laughter – 'He says "Why have a squeezy horn when you can hear the car a mile away?"'

I looked at an imposing trumpet-like affair with its nose due north and at its southern end a vast rubber bulb. This I gingerly squeezed, and the apparatus produced faithfully the sound of a goat in agony.

Three small African boys, dressed in a minimum, howled with delight.

For my edification the driver pulled up the bonnet and showed me an intricate system of strings, wire and insulating tape, keeping vital parts of the engine in position. I pointed out the leak in the radiator. He shrugged his shoulders. 'Will ulcers heal in old men?' he asked.

'*Haya!* Bwana Bishopu Yakuza' (Here comes the Bishop), said the three small boys, as they peered out from behind a pawpaw tree.

The Bishop got carefully into the car and pushed the little bolt home that kept the door from flying open. (The door's original catch had fallen off in 1934.)

'Haya Sukuma!' (Hey there, push!), called the driver.

'But why?' I asked. 'Have you no self-starter?'

'Ugh,' grunted the driver. 'Have we not the grandfather of all batteries? Push there.'

The cook, the gardener, and two wild-looking Africans with mud in their hair rushed up and pushed with all their might. With a violent explosion the old car lurched forward. The little boys fled in terror. As it rattled down the unmade road chickens flew in all directions. I came back with a Government official taking his afternoon walk. He greeted me in a rich Scottish accent. He looked at the receding cloud of dust, and turning to me said:

'What a car for a Bishop to have!'

There was a faint crash as the car went over a bump half a mile away.

We both grinned.

'He can't keep this vast job in Tanganyika going and buy a car costing more than fifty pounds,' I said.

'Aww,' said the Scotsman, 'there's no' another car like yon outside Aberdeen.'

My own bus, which served as ambulance, delivery van, and our only link with the outside world, was in the hands of George, the cheerful local garage man. His was the only car hospital for two hundred miles in any direction.

'Forty-five bob[1],' said George. 'That includes the new fan belt, blowing the grass seeds out of the radiator, and the new spare axle. I've put it under the front seat.'

'Thanks, George. We always need a spare axle on our roads.'

The Greek looked with interest at six long planks, a roll of fine chicken wire, and a coffin-like box containing spades, hoes, an axe, and great native knives for cutting a road through thorn-bush.

'Like our mud-fighting kit?' I asked.

The garage man smiled.

'You didn't tell me how you managed without a fan belt, Doc.'

'We tried spliced rope, plaited goat-skin, and finally used strips of cow-hide, wetted, and allowed to dry till they were tight. Then we came in as fast as our five working cylinders would allow. It took us seventeen hours to do the seventy miles.'

The friend from Cyprus threw back his head and roared with laughter. He waved a cheery farewell as we drove away through the crowded market. We went past Indian shops over the Cape-to-Cairo Road, where, in our car, a medical man can revise his knowledge of

---

[1] Bob - in old British money shillings were often referred to as bob - a slang term.

anatomy, or at least, of the position of most of his bones, especially two, in a thirty-mile drive.

We had just turned off the main road when we came to a deep sandy river-bed. In this part of the world rivers run for only three days in the year, but this was not one of them.

'Rush it, Bwana,' said Roger. 'It was all right yesterday.'

I dropped into low, drove quietly down the steep bank, and then accelerated briskly. We roared through the sand, and were two-thirds across when – bump – skid – stop!

Out came the jack, and the timber. Wheel after wheel was jacked up, and wood put underneath.

Crows flew cawing overhead. The herd boys were driving back their cattle to their thorn-bush enclosures.

It was nearly evening and over the hills was the miracle of an Ugogo sunset – one of the compensations of the dusty plains of East Africa.

We wiped the perspiration from our eyes, and started up. Cautiously I drove forward. The wheels gripped, and with the greatest of care I coaxed her slowly but surely to the bank, up it, and on to firm ground.

But it was only to hear the hiss of a puncture, as an iron-hard thorn found its way through the six-ply cover! This was nothing unusual. Roger fumbled for a bit of chalk, and crossed off a number on the pump box. 'The thirty-eighth puncture this month, Bwana.'

But that is just one of the joys of travel in Tanganyika.

10
Crocodile Forceps

I stood looking through the hole in the wall that served our jungle operating theatre as a window. An African nurse was carrying a bag of precious surgical instruments on her head. I felt sure they would fall. She had to go through a narrow doorway, and could she see that kerosene tin that someone had left in the middle of the path? My heart was in my mouth, but she managed everything with the greatest of ease.

All the instruments were put on shelves made from petrol boxes, placed one upon the other. As they were being put in their proper places, Daudi, my theatre attendant picked up a pair of forceps.

'What are these, Bwana?' he asked.

'Crocodile forceps,' I replied.

'What are they for?'

'Pulling beads and things out of children's ears or noses.'

'That is good weapon, Bwana. Many children put beans into their noses, or perhaps an insect walks into their ears.'

'What would the witchdoctor do, Daudi?'

'Oh, poke with thorn, Bwana, with bad effect.'

'*Kah!*' I said. 'How nice.'

The forceps sat on the shelves for a year, polished each Thursday by the theatre attendant, who delighted in watching the way in which the end of them opened and shut.

'*Kah!* It has the mouth of a cobra, Bwana.'

'Yes,' I replied, 'but it's more useful than a bag full of snakes.'

'Truly,' he laughed.

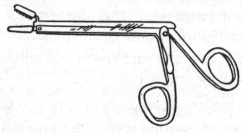

Then, one day, in the heat of the early afternoon, as I was trying to find a cool spot in my dilapidated house, a dresser arrived hot-foot.

'Bwana, a child, with a *dudu* in his ear.'

'What does he say?' asked my wife.

'Oh, a child has come to the hospital with an insect of some sort in his ear. Now I shall be able to use those crocodile forceps. I have been itching to try them out, but there has been no chance so far.'

I grabbed my topee and set out for the hospital. Under the veranda of the out-patients' department, a mere tin shed with a concrete floor, were thirty people. The sub-chief of a village some ten miles away came forward to greet me. Solemnly I shook hands with everybody, inquired after their health, their appetites, their gardens, their night's slumber and their wives, and then got down to business.

'Oh, Bwana,' said the Chief, 'my son has a *dudu* in his ear.'

'How did it get there?' I asked.

'He was lying asleep, and behold, it crawled in. And when he tried to shake it out, behold it hung on.'

An all-too-easy happening, I thought, when a child sleeps on a cow-skin on the floor in a native house that swarms with insect life. I turned back to the Chief after a hasty look round for the patient.

'Oh-o-o-o-o-e,' I said, 'and what did you do then?'

'Oh, nothing,' said the Chief.

'Liar,' breathed Daudi, behind me, in English.

'Well-er-his mother took him to the witchdoctor.'

'Ngh-h,' I said. 'And what did he do?'

'I do not know. Ask the mother.'

'Oh!' said the dresser. 'And who rules in your house? Is a woman the chief in your village?'

Everyone laughed, except the Chief, who was extremely uncomfortable.

'Come,' I said. 'Tell me all. I am no stranger to this country. Do I not know your language? Do I not understand your customs?'

'I have sinned, Bwana,' said the Chief. 'I will tell you all. I gave the witchdoctor a great bowl of millet seed and, in return, he poured medicine into my child's ear. Medicine that he made by boiling herbs and goat's fat in a little clay pot.'

'Did it work?'

'No, Bwana, it didn't!'

The patient, a lad about twelve years old, came over to me.

'Bwana,' he said. 'I'm not afraid of you. You can help me, I know.'

'How do you know?' I said.

'I remember, Bwana, the football match, when you stitched up the man's leg, and he had no pain.'

I recalled the incident when my emergency kit and some local anaesthetic had helped me to stitch up a long cut in a man's thigh at a village football match. Both the spectators and the victim were thrilled to watch the stitches put in painlessly.

I took the small lad into the operating theatre. Daudi opened the door.

'Bwana, keep my father outside. I will tell you the truth,' whispered the small boy. 'Is not the insect in my ear.'

Daudi told the relatives to wait on the veranda. The lad sat on the operating table. I collected instruments and various bottles.

'Tell me, old man, what happened.'

'I was asleep in our house, lying with my head in my blanket, on a cow-skin near the grain bin. A *dudu* crawled into my ear, and has been walking, walking,

walking ever since. I shook my head and poked round with a bit of grass, but it would not come out. My relatives tried blowing into the other ear. Then they stood me on my head, and gave me medicines to make me very sick, but the insect still walked. Then my father took me to the witchdoctor. First he poked with a thorn – *Kumbe!* How it hurt! Then he poured boiling medicine into my ear. *Yah!* How I screamed and struggled, but it did no good. My ear was burnt outside and inside, but the insect still walked – and now – my head throbs and throbs. I cannot sleep. The pain and the throbbing nearly drive me mad. Oh, Bwana, help me!'

I put some gauze soaked in cocaine over his swollen ear. It was a nasty mess! After a while the swelling had decreased and I was ready with my crocodile forceps. The dresser turned to me.

'Do it outside, Bwana. Let them all see. This is a work no witchdoctor could do. Show them our beautiful weapon. Let them see how it works, so that they may understand our better way.'

'All right,' I said, and we moved our kit out on the ward veranda. With a special torch adapted for looking into the ear, I proceeded to locate the insect before the admiring relatives, who crowded round. The little boy kept backing away.

'Keep your head still, my son,' I said.

'I'm trying, Bwana, but it just moves all by itself.'

We tried again.

'It's hard, Bwana. Let me put my head against the wall, and then, behold, I cannot move it.'

We moved over into a corner. He sat on one small stool and I on another. First I cleaned the ear with a wisp of wool, and put in some soothing drops. The relatives watched everything open-mouthed. Gently I removed clots and dirt that gave ample evidence of the witchdoctor's thoroughness with his thorn.

'Hurting you, my son?' I asked.

'Yes, Bwana, but only a very little bit.'

My auriscope – the ear torch – at last could be put into the ear, and peering along its lighted barrel I could see part of the insect. I groped for it with the forceps.

'Ya-a-a-a-a,' said the boy, 'the *dudu* is walking.'

'Truly,' I replied. 'It's his last walk, though.'

'Can you see him, Bwana?'

'Yes, but quietly for a minute, and I'll have him out. Hold your breath.'

Again I sighted the insect, and grabbed.

'Nearly,' I breathed, and then – 'Got him!'

In triumph I produced the offender firmly gripped in the jaws of the forceps.

'Ya-a-a-a-a-a,' said the relatives.

'He-e-e-e-e,' said the small boy, rubbing his ear tenderly. 'Give it to me, Bwana. Let me have it.'

I released the jaws of the forceps, and the small boy took the insect and ground it between his thumb-nails with great thoroughness.

'There!' he said.

Everybody roared with laughter. The Chief shook me firmly by the hand.

'Ati Muwaha' (well Chief), said Daudi, 'could you get rid of this insect yourself? Or could the witchdoctor – by your own efforts?'

'*Hamba hadodo*' (Not even a little bit), said the small boy, feelingly. 'But the Bwana could, with his crocodile forceps.'

'*Yah*,' said Daudi. 'That *dudu* is like sin. You cannot rid yourself of it, no matter how hard you try. Only Jesus Christ, the Son of God, who loved you and gave Himself for you, can do that.'

The crowd of Africans whispered excitedly together, but the small boy came across to me, and said:

'Bwana, when I am chief, I will see that everyone comes to hospital.'

He was silent for a moment, and then, rather wistfully, he said:

'Bwana, when I have been to school, may I come here to learn to be a dresser like Daudi?'

Some years later a young man approached me in the hospital compound.

'Do you remember me, Bwana?'

I looked at him hard. 'Yes, but I can't quite remember where I saw you last.'

He grinned, and ground his thumbs together.

'Do you remember me now, Bwana?'

'Surely,' I said. 'You had a *dudu* in your ear.'

'Yes, Bwana. And because of what you did to me that day, and what you told me, I have become a Christian and next year I'm coming to hospital to be a dresser, so that I can help others as you helped me.'

11
Leprosy

Daudi was sitting on a high stool in the dispensary, while his junior deftly cut a parting in his tightly-curled hair with an ancient safety razor blade. I grinned as I put my head round the door and watched proceedings.

The barber looked up.

'Our hair is easier to do than yours, Bwana. Once cut a furrow in it, and the parting's there for days. African hair is also better than European, because, with many of the Bwanas, their hair is only a memory.'

'Tell me, Daudi. Why do the women shave their heads here?'

Both the dressers laughed.

'So would you, Bwana, if you lived as they live, in dirty houses swarming with insects. You see, when there is no hair, what can the insects hold on to?'

I laughed, and was just settling down on the dispensary table to discuss at length values of different varieties of hair-dressing, when two gaunt little figures appeared at the door.

'*Zo wuswero wenyu*' (Good evening), said the larger of the two.

'*Ale zo wuswero wenyu nyenye*' (Good evening to you both) we all replied in one breath.

Daudi turned to me, and in English said:

'We don't need a microscope to diagnose them, Bwana!'

They were indeed a wretched-looking pair, each dressed only in a rag, their ribs protruding painfully, and their faces gnarled with the ravages of leprosy. I got to my feet, and went towards them, putting a hand on a shoulder of each.

'Tell me, my children, where do you come from?'

'We used to live at Idifu, Bwana, out there beyond the thorn-bush forest,' said one, his little voice raised in pitch to indicate the distance he had travelled.

'About ten miles away, Bwana,' said Daudi. 'It's a very heathen place.'

'Where do you live now?' I asked.

'Oh, we sleep in the forest, Bwana. We have no other place. Our father will not have us because we have this skin disease.'

'Do they know, Daudi?' I asked in English. 'Do they realise they have leprosy?'

'I think so, Bwana.'

The little boy suddenly sat down and burst into tears.

'Oh my mother,' he wailed. 'I am so hungry. We have travelled so far, and my feet ache so.'

His elder brother helped me to pick him up and comfort him.

'Nobody wants us, Bwana. We have gone to all our relatives, but they do nothing but say: "There is no room for you here." They are all afraid of the disease. They want us to die. They sent us out to the forest, and hoped the hyenas would get us.'

I turned to my African friend.

'They are almost starving, Daudi. We will have to feed them up a bit before we do anything else. Give them a great big dish of *wugali* (porridge). I will send them up some soup as well.'

'Will they sleep in the leper treatment hut, Bwana?'

'Yes, Daudi, we will let them each have one of those old blankets. See that they are bathed and looked after, there's a good chap.'

'All right, Bwana, I'll fix it. Here's a chance for us to show them something of the love of Jesus. We are not afraid of this disease, and we definitely can help them. Notice, Bwana, that the witchdoctor would not even try to do anything for them.'

'Huh,' said Samson. 'Does he not say: "Is there any profit in a leper?"'

'Anyhow, we shall be able to take them up to the C.M.S. Leprosy Settlement at Makutupora on Thursday, on the way up north.'

'Bwana,' said the small child. 'Will you, too, send us away?'

'No, my son,' I said. 'We shall help you. We have a little house for you here where you can stay till we go in a motor-car to the place where your disease is cured.'

'But, Bwana, we have no food. We have no blankets. We are poor ones,' said the elder.

'I shall give you each a blanket, and you shall eat till you can eat no more.'

'Y-a-a-a-a-a,' they both said. 'Y-a-a-a-a-a!'

They took me by the hand, and I led them to the little treatment hut.

'Can we stay here,' they asked, 'in this nice little house? It is so clean.'

I laughed. 'Yes, you stay here. There are mats for you to sleep on. Daudi will bring you food. First you must bath.'

'But, Bwana, we are too tired to carry water from the well.'

'We shall bring you hot water and soap,' I said.

Then I sat down beside them on the stone step, and told them how Jesus had healed people who had the same disease as theirs, and how Jesus gives life and joy that lasts for ever, when He takes away not only the leprosy of our skins, but the leprosy of our souls.

'Bwana, can you get leprosy in your heart, like I've got in my fingers?' said the little boy, lifting his hand which already was affected by the disease.

'It's worse than that,' I said. 'Leprosy of your heart is sin. It's such a bad thing that God sent His own Son to take it away, and He died to do that.'

'How did He die, Bwana?'

'Men nailed Him to a tree,' I replied. 'Drove nails through His hands and through His feet. He hung there until He died.'

'To take away our sin?' they asked.

'Yes,' I replied. 'To take away your sin and mine.'

A nurse arrived with a plate heaped with native porridge, and a big dish of boiled beans.

'Oh, thank you, Bwana,' they said. 'Are we not hungry? Do our stomachs not stick to our backbones?'

The elder one looked up at me.

'Bwana, did God send you here?'

'He did,' I replied.

'Then will you tell Him that we are thankful, and that we want to hear more about His Son?'

The little chap was contentedly cramming his mouth as full as he could. I left them as they made short work of the meal.

I carefully washed my hands in the ward.

'There is not much danger of getting leprosy, if you're clean.'

'No, Bwana, but think of all the children in a dirty hut, without any air, all lying on the same mat. Do you wonder the disease spreads like a bush-fire?'

Later that evening, as I did a round of the hospital beds, I went to see our two little friends. Daudi was just burning their filthy loin cloths on the end of a thorn twig. The children were sound asleep, rolled up in some old blankets.

'Poor children,' said Daudi. 'They were dirty. I made them bath twice!'

For three days they lived in the little hut, eating their fill, and cheerfully playing with an old tennis ball. Each day they stood on a big stone and bathed by dipping warm water from a kerosene tin with a gourd and pouring it over one another's heads. They were dressed in little white shirts, and Daudi had neatly bandaged their diseased fingers.

Thursday arrived. The truck was loaded with all sorts of surgical instruments, medicines and ointments, and there were two sacks full of bandages. Sitting cheerfully in the back, on an upturned petrol box, were our two little friends, each clutching a bag of food for the journey. At first they were a little frightened at the bumping of the car – they had never been in one before. Soon, however, they were howling with delight as we struggled through the thick sand, and pushed our way through the jungle. We jolted along the Cape-to-Cairo Road. Clouds of red dust blew into the car. At long last we reached Dodoma. I was most amused to see the little boys liberally coated in pink dust. Their eyes opened wide as they saw the people of the town.

'*Yah*,' said one, as he watched three Englishmen walking along the street. 'Who'd have thought that there were so many Europeans in the world?'

'*Kah*,' said the other. 'Look at the Indians. The world is a big place, truly!'

I presented each of them with a great lump of sticky brown sugar. They looked at it doubtfully.

'Is it medicine, Bwana? Has it a fierce taste?'

'Try it and see,' I replied.

Gingerly they complied, and their smiles cracked the dust on their faces.

'*Yah*,' said they. 'It is good!'

We drove on out of the town, over the thorn-bush plains, past great piles of granite boulders, that looked as though some giant's child had been playing blocks, past shallow lakes covered with bird-life, and then up a gradual slope through dense forest. About twenty baboons dashed chattering across the road. My little friends clapped their hands and held their sides with laughter. Before us stretched mile after mile of dazzling white salt plains, and then we came to the foot of a steep line of hills – the Rift Wall. It was a perilous drive up a narrow unfenced pass. Four hundred feet below lay the wreckage of a lorry, whose driver had made a slight error of judgment. The little boys clung tightly to the edge of the car, peering down over the sheer face of the cliff. The engine boiled explosively, but one could not stop on that hill. It was with a feeling of relief that I swung to the right and pulled up at a white house which stood on the top of the cliff. Out we all climbed, and I went forward to grip the hand of my colleague, Dr Wallace, who is spending his life looking after people with leprosy.

'Two boarders for you, Wallace. These two chaps are from Mvumi way.'

My friend walked across to them, and shook their hands.

'Will you stay with me,' he said, 'and let me help your sickness?'

One of them turned to me.

'Will they feed us here Bwana, like you fed us? And will they be kind to us like you were at Mvumi?'

I smiled at Wallace over his head.

'Oh, yes,' I said. 'This is a C.M.S. Hospital, and the Bwana here will look after you much better than we could.'

'Oh,' they said, 'and can he tell us about Jesus?'

'That's why I'm here,' he smiled.

He called one of his dressers.

'Benjamin, take these two lads to the boys' hospital and fix them up. Put them on treatment Number 3. I will be down to see them later.'

Turning to me, he said: 'Tea, as usual?' and turning to his cook: 'The very big tea-pot. You know the Bwana's thirst!'

We stood on his veranda, looking out over the plains. Pegged out in the shade was the skin of an enormous lion, at least nine feet from tip to toe.

'Did you shoot that lion?' I asked.

'Yes. I'm becoming a famous hunter. They told me that there were pigs in the sweet potatoes, but when I got there, that is what I found. He was so close I couldn't miss him. It was just as well I didn't, because he was only fifteen yards away when I pulled the trigger! It's a nice skin, all the same.'

Mrs Wallace poured out the tea. She had been a C.M.S. welfare worker in Egypt, and was now looking after the healthy children of leprosy patients.

'Seven new babies, Doctor, since you were here last,' she said, as I helped myself to sugar. 'All as healthy as can be; not a trace of the disease.'

'That's good,' I said. 'How does the segregation scheme get on?'

'Splendidly,' said my colleague. 'You see, all the infected folk are in the colony in the valley, and the symptom-free and healthy people are put here on the crest. When you've finished your third cup, we'll go and have a look at the settlement.'

I looked with amazement at the work that was being done. Wallace was not only preacher and physician to these folk, but he had planned a hundred ways of helping them in other phases of their lives. I passed carpenters' shops where they were making native beds, chairs, and a hundred and one gadgets for their own use. An old man in an advanced stage of the disease, without fingers or toes, was skilfully rolling rope between his palm and his thigh. He smiled up at me.

'There are many things you can do, Bwana, even if you've got no fingers.'

As we walked on, Wallace said: 'I encourage them to do things. Leprosy's a lazy disease, and if they have nothing to do, they progressively get worse. Find them a job that they can do, and they are as happy as can be. With treatment, and good diet, very many of them become symptom-free.'

I looked at the saw-pits, where men were industriously cutting up timber to build further huts for patients.

'That man over there, using the cross-cut saw, looked hopeless three years ago, but in three months he will be able to go out symptom-free. He was thin and weak when he came, but we gave him graduated exercise and good food – and look at him now.'

'Paulo,' he called. '*Njo*' (Come here).

I recognised the man as an advanced case which I had seen shortly after my arrival in Africa, but I looked in vain for the great yellow patch of the disease that had revealed his leprosy.

Paulo gripped my hand. 'I'm strong now, Bwana, and nearly well. Also I'm now an expert at wood-cutting. It is here that the whole outlook of my life has been changed.'

We had just reached the gardens and I was looking at the pumpkins and green vegetables, and the mango trees that were flourishing near the spring. Wallace said to me:

'That man, Paulo, when he came here, was called "Chibedi."'

'That's Gogo for disobedience,' I laughed.

'He wasn't misnamed, either,' said Wallace. 'He was a real pain in the neck to start with, but when he came to Jesus Christ, it turned him inside out. Did you know he ran the services here last Sunday? There's no humbug about his Christian life.'

'It's a worth-while job, all right, Wallace, from every point of view.'

'I know it's my own job, but frankly you can't help being enthusiastic when you see the sting being drawn from leprosy. And you can give people a new basis for their health, and the solid foundation of Christian faith which means everything to us. Look at those huts, every one of them a simple, cheap and effective way of maintaining family life and yet treating the disease. The healthy children up on the hill can see their parents, yet there is no danger of their contracting the disease. Here, too, people have their own gardens, and we can make sure they get enough food and regular treatment.'

'What's the cost of each one of the little cottages?'

'Fifty pounds builds the place and maintains it for ten years and five pounds is the average yearly cost for the upkeep of each of our people.'

I whistled.

'Probably each one you've got here prevents dozens from being infected in the villages.'

'It certainly does,' he replied.

We walked back in silence up the hill.

Two years elapsed, and once again I was drinking tea with Wallace.

'Who's your new house-boy?' I asked.

'Don't you recognise him, White? He's the bigger of the two lads you brought to me two years ago. He is symptom-free now, and a most promising youngster. He has completely justified every penny we have spent on him, and he's a thorough-going Christian.'

I turned to the lad.

'Where is your little brother? Is he also well now?'

His eyes filled with tears.

'He's gone to be with God. The disease had gone too far… But he wasn't frightened, Bwana. He knew where he was going… There is no fear in death when you are a friend of the Lord Jesus, and you know He is waiting to welcome you.'

12
A Duck or a Goose

I cleaned out the ancient gun, and oiled it. Somehow I felt a duck or a goose would go well for Sunday lunch. I pocketed four cartridges, and thought to myself: 'A cup of tea first and then I'll see to dinner!'

I called Roger, and picked up a three-months old Australian newspaper. I looked up from the advertisements (the only thing I hadn't read at least twice), and nearly dropped the paper in my amazement. There was the cook boy dressed only in one of my wife's aprons.

'Whatever are you doing in that?' I said.

'It's Saturday, Bwana. I'm washing my clothes. I have only one shirt, and one pair of shorts. So I borrowed Bibi's apron. I'm saving every shilling to buy the cows for my dowry. Did I tell you my relatives at Nghali have agreed to give me three cows – that makes sixteen. Only four to get now.'

I could see his broad back – all of it – in the mirror – and laughed to myself.

'That's splendid, Roger. Make some tea, and we'll celebrate, and then, shall we shoot some geese?' I asked. 'I have borrowed Bwana Shamba's (The Government Agricultural Officer's) gun, and I thought we would try to get a duck for tomorrow's dinner.'

'Yah!' said Roger. 'I'll go!'

It was a three-mile walk to the shallow lake. Roger had borrowed the cook's third-best shorts, and the school-teacher's green football jersey.

We walked through the native village followed by an admiring group of small boys, then across a wide sandy river-bed, and through a mango garden. In front of us between two cone-shaped hills that rose sharply out of the plains was a shallow reed-fringed lake. We passed the ruins of an old Arab house, and turned down a narrow path between great leafless baobabs. We walked round the edge of the shallow lake past water holes where humped-back cattle were drinking, and Gogo women were filling their gourds. They looked at my gun, and smiled:

'Meat, Bwana?'

'We hope so,' I replied.

There was a splendid place on the very edge of the lake, in tall reeds. We crouched there and waited for the geese to come back after their raiding excursions on the peanut gardens. The sun was setting in the blaze of colour that is characteristic of these dusty Ugogo plains. We stood watching the teeming bird-life of the lake. Overhead flew a long irregular line of white egret, the sun glinting on them and making them look like silver as they flew over the baobabs and out of sight. Half a dozen coot swam into a little bay in the reeds, and seeing us, departed faster than they had come! Seven great, ungainly golden-crested crane flapped their great wings as they settled in the tree-tops. Roger grabbed my arm.

'Here they come, Bwana.'

We crouched out of sight. Overhead, in correct formation, came a long-angled gaggle of geese. I fired both barrels. Roger leapt to his feet with a yell, and plunged through the mud after one of the birds. There was a definite satisfaction in seeing your Sunday's dinner fall like a stone a few yards away. The air seemed full of birds. The report of the gun created a great commotion. All sorts and sizes of water-fowl flew screaming to the far end of the lake. A very muddy, but cheerful Roger returned in a moment or two grasping a goose by the neck.

'Two in two shots, Bwana. It's the first time you've ever done that!'

'Well, Roger, I couldn't do it again. Would you like to have a shot?'

'*Yah*,' he said. 'Would I?'

We could hear another gaggle honking in the distance. Roger crouched, balancing on one foot, the gun pointing skywards. I pushed over the safety-catch and said:

'Aim about a yard in front of the one you want to hit.'

Roger rolled his eyes with excitement, and said: '*Yah!*'

The birds came within range. Roger leaned farther back, and pulled the trigger. The gun roared. The birds flew on safely! Then I looked down to see Roger on his back. The kick of the gun had over-balanced him, and there he lay, in the mud, weak with laughter, the gun on top of him!

'Truly,' he said, 'we should live on chicken all our days if I had to work that *nhuti* that kicks like an angry donkey.'

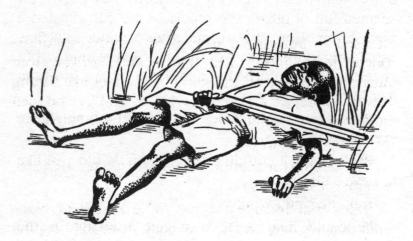

13
Fighting Mud and Fever

'It used to be quite a nice piano,' said one Jungle Doctor to his friend, who had recently arrived from Australia to carry on the job. 'I don't feel like tuning it with a spanner and screw-wrench, and I've no idea how to replace the felt that the *dudus* have eaten.'

'What's a *dudu*?'

'It's Swahili for anything that crawls, bites, or grips, whether it's big or small.'

'Does that include the big route march of black ants that we saw on the way back from the hospital today?'

'Yes, and scorpions, ticks, ear-wigs, centipedes, mosquitoes, anything and everything.'

'Africa seems literally to swarm with *dudus*, then?'

'It certainly does. I once saw an unfortunate missionary walking through thick grass. He didn't see a *safari* (a regular trek) of red ants that the people call "Siafu." Suddenly I saw him leap up, wrench off his shirt and yell, as he made frantic efforts to pull off the fiercely biting insects. He looked terribly funny up there. I laughed till my sides ached, and was so preoccupied that I didn't see them approaching me, and before I was aware of them, I was staging my own little side-show.'

'H'm…. Cheery spot, this.'

'No doubt about it. Have you ever heard of a mango fly?'

'Never! What's it like? Sort of fruit fly?'

'No, it's a very real catch for an unfortunate medico. I was staying down near the Tanganyika coast with young David. We hung out his clothes to dry, but somehow, one of his small shirts got on to the line without being washed. This was real joy for the mango fly, who proceeded to lay eggs surreptitiously. Three days later the little chap was covered with boils – or what I thought were boils – so I treated them in the usual way, but imagine my horror when, a day or two later, one burst, and out popped a vigorous maggot. And then I operated on the rest of the forty-three. It's a horrid memory.'

'Definitely nasty, I should think!'

'Well, it's been a big day. Let's turn in. You never know what the night will hold. First, I'll brew a cup of tea. While I'm fixing the primus, give us a tune. Push the soft pedal half-way down, and avoid any key involving B Flat, near Middle C, and it'll sound slightly less worse!'

The tea was duly disposed of. We said 'Good night,' and I was just about in bed when a loud and rather frightened voice called 'Hodi?' I opened the door.

With a spear and two sticks in one hand, and a smoky lantern in the other, my visitor came in.

'*Mbukwa* (Good evening), Bwana.'

'*Mbukwa*' (Good evening).

'I have brought a letter from Suliman, the Indian at Handari.'

He handed me the second stick, which was split, and in the middle of it was a soiled envelope. I couldn't help smiling as I looked at the messenger, with his cow-skin sandals, and a cheap calico shirt, which he wore outside his threadbare shorts. Right across his chest was a rampant dragon, apparently suffering from acute indigestion, and beneath it was printed: 'Forty-two yards. C quality. Made in Japan.' I remembered the hospital sewing-boy had told me that there was a reduction of 2d.[1] on shirts made from that portion of the roll of material that had the trade-mark on it!

I pulled out and read the letter:

Handari, Tanganyika.

Dear Bwana Doctor,

I finds myself and wife in the troubles, the later has fevers (103) together with shivering and perspirations. Come please just now.

I have the honour to remain sir,
Your obedient servant,
Suliman Ludha.

---

[1] 2d - In the old British currency prior to decimilisation the shorthand for pennies was the letter d.

119

My friend read it over my shoulder.

'Here's fun and games, Doc. Especially after that hour-and-a-half's rain we had last night.'

I nodded, and turned to the messenger.

'Go to the hospital. Call Roger, and tell him to load the car with spades, hoes, chains, rope – all the things we use in fighting mud.'

'Yes, Bwana.'

We both dressed in our oldest clothes, filled up the hurricane lantern with kerosene, and Dr Hannah produced a miniature torch which he thought might be useful. We checked over syringes, needles, and the various drugs in the emergency kit, and squelched through sun-dried mud to the brick shed where lived our Ford. Roger had just put in a thirty-foot coil of rope, and was grinning from ear to ear.

'We'll have fun tonight, Bwana! I hear the rivers are running.'

I started up, only waiting for the messenger to scramble up beside the cook boy in the back. The headlights seemed to cut a path through the intense darkness. Night-birds, dazzled, fluttered against the windscreen. Ahead of us were four donkeys in the middle of the road. They kicked up their heels and trotted off as I blew the horn. We moved through the native village. Here and there men sat round the red embers of a fire, talking, or playing a variety of African draughts. On each side of us were millet fields. The heads, heavy with grain, made an archway to pass under. Occasionally I ducked as one of these, bent over by the rain, hit the wind-screen. Then we were in a cleared area near the river. I stopped, with the headlights focused on a brown stream of water. I took off my boots and socks and waded carefully in to test the bottom. Roger was with me, and said:

'It couldn't be better, Bwana, only three inches deep, and the sand is hard as concrete.'

On the far side the bank had to be dug down. In five minutes we were back in the car, and moved slowly across, rushing only when we came to the last ten yards, to get up the sudden steepness of the bank.

'That's one,' I said. 'Twelve to go.'

The next four were plain sailing. We climbed a hill, covered with thorn-bush and suddenly into the lane of light before us burst six gazelle. They were most disconcerted and bounded ahead of us in great leaps for at least half a mile. I almost forgot the state of the road in the exhilaration of watching them.

Directly in front loomed another river. I knew by experience we would have no trouble, so I dropped into low gear, and rushed it. Spray flew everywhere, and I was relieved to feel the wheels bite firmly into the bank. We were on the top again. But immediately ahead was a deep black gash in the road. We got out to have a look. Storm waters had cut a four-foot deep V-shaped gutter right through a corn-field, and the road. It was useless to try to fill it up, the only thing to do was to dig it out. We all got to work digging out the sides, until I felt we could get through.

'Roger, you and the messenger push – and push with all your strength when I blow the horn. We'll only just get through! Whatever you do, push, or we'll get stuck.'

I backed the car, and took a run at the ditch. I blew the horn, Roger and Dr Hannah pushed, but the messenger fled! There was a grinding of metal. The car slewed sideways and stopped, with the engine still going, the wheels digging deeply into the soft mud of the bank. We were stuck! I got out to view the damage. I think we could have done it if that fellow had pushed! But now, there we were – the car suspended with three of its wheels in the air, and the bumper-bars carrying the whole weight of the vehicle.

In the confusion, the messenger crept back, grabbed his lantern and spear, and made off unnoticed. We dug a little and had a try to get out. It was no use. So we held a council of war.

'Suliman can speak English of a sort. We're only two miles away from his shop now. I suggest you push on, Hannah, and see what you can do for the patient. Roger and I will get out of this somehow. Be careful to keep along the track, or you will fall into a swamp or two. Messy places!'

Dr Hannah packed the emergency case under his arm, and set out, picking his way by the light of his diminutive torch, while Roger and I took off the bumper-bars.

'Now we've got to find stone to put under the wheels, something that will hold firm, and not let us slip. You take the lamp.'

Roger took the lantern, and walked off up the creek. He came back carrying a huge stone. I lay under the car, and in the dark jacked up the wheel, and with a tyre lever dug out a hole to put the stone into. Roger was bringing the stones at a great rate. It looked as though we'd be out in half an hour, when I heard a crash, and a roar of laughter. It was as dark as the inside of a cow!

'What's up?' I called.

I switched on the headlights, and trudging towards me, weak with laughter, came Roger, holding the remains of my hurricane lantern. He was soaking wet.

'I slipped in the mud, Bwana, fell on the lantern, and broke it. Look… but it doesn't matter much, because it was your lantern, and these are my brother's trousers!'

We spent at least another hour fishing round in the darkness of the river-bed for stones, Roger telling me all the time how prevalent snakes were in this area. At long last the track of stones under the wheels was finished.

'Nothing like stone. You'll slip on mud, but not on stone. Just like our faith in Jesus, Bwana. You can trust Him.'

'True, Roger. Let's just ask His help before we have a go at getting out.'

We were a very dilapidated pair, but as we knelt by the running-board, we were conscious that even there, in the darkness of East Africa, we were very close to God. I opened the door, and started up. Roger got behind to push. I let in the clutch, and in one bound we were out!

'Hey!!!' yelled Roger, from behind. He jumped in beside me.

'Wonder what's happened to Bwana Hannah!'

'He'll have been there and finished the work by now,' I said.

'I wonder!' said Roger – but we didn't for long. A mile further down the road in a place piled high with granite boulders, sitting on the root of a great baobab, with a stone in each hand, was my friend. We pulled up.

'What's up?'

'I was trying to save the battery, and didn't see this root. I tripped over it and broke the torch bulb. I've been here for an hour; a family of hyenas is taking a lively interest in me, too!'

I backed the car. The headlights showed some hyenas skulking not twenty yards away!

Ten minutes later we pulled up in front of the Indian's shop, and walked in through the corrugated iron door. On each side, piled pell-mell, were bicycle pumps, brown sugar, bags of beans, and an indescribable medley of stuff. We went through the shop to a bedroom. Lying on a low couch covered by a cheap Japanese mosquito net, was an Indian girl. She was certainly extremely ill. Hannah and I consulted together in low voices.

'I think we'd better give her an injection of quinine into a vein.'

'I agree,' said my friend. 'But I forgot to tell you that, when I fell over, I broke the syringe!'

'Well, we'll have to give her quinine by mouth and hope for the best. There's nothing else to be done.'

The pills were duly swallowed. Roger was sitting in front of the fire-place, built some three feet off the ground. He had insisted that tea should be made for his Bwana, who, he said, had been paddling in much mud, and therefore required it!

Hearing that we were in the town, another Indian asked me to see his wife, who had asthma. She was duly dealt with. It was just after 4 a.m. when we set out to return. Suliman lent me a lantern, and a powerful torch. Our farewells were cut short by vivid lightning and crashing thunder. We had just crossed the first river, when frantic knocking in the back of the car made me pull up.

'Look, Bwana,' said Roger, pointing upstream.

I switched the torch in the direction he indicated, and saw a foaming breaker come rolling down the hills. In a few seconds the river we had just crossed was a swirling mass of turbid water.

'Hmmm...!' said Dr Hannah. 'Just in time!'

With the greatest of care we approached the scene of our former struggles. Stones were re-adjusted, but this time, although we skidded back twice, we managed to get through.

'*Nzogolo*,' said Roger. 'The second cock crow. Time for me to get up!'

'What did he say?' asked my colleague.

'He says it's time to get up!'

'Does he? Well, it's bed and blankets for me,' said Dr Hannah.

14
Meningitis

'*Kumbe!* It was a bargain, Bwana. Two cows for nineteen shillings. I only got them because old Muchiwa had to find his shillings to pay his poll tax.'

My cook boy stuttered in his excitement.

'Only two more, and then I can get married.'

'That's splendid, Roger. And now I suppose you want to go and tell Nora?'

'Please, Bwana, and Daudi says you are going to the Buigiri on safari. May I go, too? I'm sure I can get those two cows from my relatives who live near there.'

'But who'll do your work here, Roger?'

'School has broken up, Bwana, and Anthony knows the cook boy's job.'

'Very well, if the cook agrees, you can come with us when we set out tomorrow at sunrise.'

The car was being loaded with all sorts of medicines for our branch hospital, twenty miles away. Daudi, the dispenser, helped me as I checked over lists of drugs and dressings.

'Everything's here, Bwana, except a hundred-

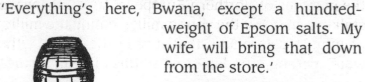

weight of Epsom salts. My wife will bring that down from the store.'

'*Kah*,' I said. 'Will she not break in the middle? Is she not terribly thin?'

Daudi smiled. 'Get it on her head, Bwana, and she'll carry it all day!'

A few minutes later the keg arrived, carefully balanced on the head of the slight African girl. Her infant son peered interestedly at us over her shoulder. I couldn't help smiling when I saw that Nora, Roger's fiancée, had come 'in case her companion had trouble with her load on the way down to the hospital!' She coyly covered her head till all was ready, but, as I climbed into the driver's seat, she moved close to the car, and shook hands ceremoniously with Roger, whispering something and smiling. I winked at the windscreen wiper, slipped in the clutch, and we moved off through the village.

We had to cross seventy rivers in the twenty-eight miles' drive between the hospitals. As we drove through the gardens that lined the apology for a road, we saw thousands of ibis that regularly migrate from the marshes of Northern Europe to Africa. Many were stalking amongst the young millet, eating the millions of minute caterpillars that invade the crops. Others were swirling round in great spirals high in the air.

'*Yah*,' said Roger. 'The *yobwa* are our best friends. If it were not for them, we should have no crops. There is no Mugogo who would dare to kill one of them.'

Coming round a granite outcrop we almost ran into a dozen great apes sunning themselves on the road. They chattered and squealed and swung off into the thornbush.

We were still laughing at the incident when we came to a group of Wagogo standing beside the road. I pulled up and greeted them':

'*Mbukweni*.'

'*Mbukwa*, Bwana,' they replied.

'What are you discussing?'

An old man shook his head.

'There's great danger in the country, Bwana. Are we not moving? The country is bewitched.'

I questioned them further, but they only said:

'We must move. There is black magic.'

They walked on, a disconsolate collection of people, leaving their mud houses behind. A couple of skinny chickens scratched forlornly outside the derelict huts amongst the rubbish. Scores of crows were walking round, looking for scraps of food. From all the country

I could see little processions of people; women carrying what they could of their worldly goods on their heads, and the men herding their skinny flocks, and driving them away from their homes. Always the same story 'Magic. We have been bewitched! Black magic!' And then a mutter that I could not completely understand about Death.

An hour later we arrived at the branch hospital. I went up to the ward, while Roger unpacked the car, and carried out bottles and tins of drugs, ointments, pills, injections, and all the commonplace doings of a bush hospital. When I returned to the dispensary he was pouring castor-oil into narrow-necked bottles from a kerosene tin. All his muscles were taut, and every faculty was centred on directing that oily stream into – and not onto – the bottle.

'Don't laugh, Bwana,' he gasped, 'or my hand will shake. H-e-e-e-e. That was work!' he said, as the last drops went in the right direction. 'Now may I have three days off for my cow hunt?'

'Go your hardest,' I said, 'but be back by Friday at noon.'

'I will, Bwana. Good-bye and thank you.'

He picked up the battered topee that had once been mine, and walked off round the hill where I had seen my first leopard.

I was discussing the meningitis epidemic with the Sister.

'There certainly is meningitis in the village, Doctor. I know of over a dozen deaths already. They don't come into the hospital. They put the whole thing down to witch-craft, and the medicine men are terribly busy smelling out witches, and manufacturing charms.'

I had a hectic day in that little mud-and-wattle dispensary with its cupboards and tables made from petrol boxes and its bowls and buckets contrived from petrol tins. I examined patients, treated eyes, viewed some fifty babies that had been brought by their proud mothers for my inspection, and finally, pulled out some of the inevitable teeth. By the end of the day there were at least a dozen folk who wanted to travel back to Mvumi with me. I made four cases for operation as comfortable as I could in the back, and took two stalwarts to push, in case we struck trouble in the rivers. It was late at night when we arrived at Mvumi, but I found the old African clergyman waiting for me.

'Bwana, I have heard a rumour that they have the disease of death in the village beyond the thorn-tree forest. This is a very serious matter.'

'Tell me of this disease, Mika.'

He shook his head.

'Bwana, nothing can be done for it. When a man gets it he almost always dies, and even if his body should recover, is his mind not dead? Is there any profit in his life then, when he acts all day like a monkey?'

'Why should people die, Mika? I have the answer to this disease. I have pills and injections that will cure it.'

'Not the disease of death, Bwana. It isn't just malaria, you know! In this sickness, people get bad fever, their necks become stiff, they become unconscious, and rave, and then they die. We have never heard of a cure for this.'

'There is a cure, though, and I have it here. We call this disease meningitis, and these pills here – look at them – will cure it!'

In his excitement, he got to his feet.

'Bwana, let me send messengers at once to the chiefs to tell them this great news. But are you absolutely sure they are a cure, Bwana?'

'I'm certain, but tell the chiefs that it is essential to bring the people in early – at the very first sign – directly their necks show any stiffness.'

'Yes, Bwana. I understand.'

He sat down and wrote note after note. He folded the last one, and put it carefully in a split stick.

'Bwana, the hospital will overflow. People will come from everywhere. What a parable this is. Is this not just what Jesus did? Your pills are the only way to save people's lives from this deadly meningitis, and Jesus' death is the only way to save people's souls from sin. Native medicine can do nothing, and the witchdoctor is beaten, but your pills will destroy the power of this disease, just as Jesus is the only One who can destroy the soul-poison – sin.'

'That is so, Mika. That's why I feel our medical missions help us to preach a Gospel that even the bush folk who can't read can understand.'

Runners went all over the country, and soon from all quarters patients came pouring in. Little processions of people arrived at the hospital, some being carried, others being almost dragged along. It was pathetic to see the eagerness with which they came for help. Our bed space was absolutely inadequate. We had cleared out the store-room and sent home all but our most serious cases. Convalescents slept in the kitchen, fracture people were put in the training room, the children's ward was emptied of beds, and mats put on the floor in their place. Nurses ran to and fro with blankets and sheets. In the dispensary Samson prepared M. & B. in salt solution. He checked over new syringes and needles, and prepared them for immediate use. Daudi was cleaning slides in the pathology room, and over a spirit-lamp he sterilised test-tubes that would shortly hold the spinal fluid of epidemic patients. In the theatre Kefa prepared trays for urgent operation, and a long needle used to drain off this fluid from the spine of the patient. Primuses were filled and sterilisers taken to each ward. I sat in my office and carefully drew up a routine. Everything had to be done with the greatest of care. No step could be forgotten, or life would be lost.

I shall never forget the first patient. The disease was far advanced. He was unconscious and delirious. One of the men who carried him in, grumbled:

'*Kah*, it's wasted effort to carry him in six miles. Will he not be dead before sunset?'

The relatives sat together outside the laboratory window talking in muffled whispers.

Our whole routine was moving smoothly. Daudi took a blood slide and brought a special test-tube. Kefa brought a needle to tap the spine, while the dispenser produced a syringe, needles, and M. & B. tablets. A minor operation was performed. The fluid from his spine was cloudy, and Daudi reported:

'No malaria parasites seen in the blood.'

At once I gave a very large injection.

Daudi touched me on the shoulder.

'Can he live, Bwana?' he whispered.

'I think so. He is in God's hands; let's pray about it.'

A minute or two later we got up from our knees.

'As I looked through the microscope, Bwana, I heard his relatives discussing how they would divide up his cows when he died. They feel certain that he cannot possibly recover.'

'Whatever you do, Daudi, don't let them come into the ward until I say the word.'

I turned to the dressers.

'Everyone must wear his mask all the time that he is in the ward. I don't want any of you to get this disease.'

I gave a further injection that night. Next morning I was amazed to see the man lying in bed, conscious, and dealing effectively with a large plate of native porridge. Daudi was jubilant!

'Will not his relatives get a shock when they see him? They are waiting in the village till he dies. Then they will howl with their voices, but in their hearts they will be thinking of his cows...'

A rather truculent Mugogo, with mud in his hair, and with a long, razor-sharp spear, came up to us.

'Bwana, we demand to see our relative. We know he is dying, and we want to be round his bedside when he dies.'

Daudi trod gently on my toe.

'The Bwana says you may come to the ward, but you must all wear bandages round your faces, and be sprayed with germ-killer.'

Four men and an evil-looking old woman all lined up to be sprayed with an insecticide gun, and have bits of bandage tied none too gently over their noses and mouths.

'Oh, our poor relative,' said one man.

'*Yayagwe*,' groaned the others.

'Come and have a look at him,' said Daudi, 'and don't make a noise.'

'*Kah*,' said the leader, as he walked behind the screen, and saw his relation with a handful of porridge half-way to his mouth.'

They stood dumbfounded.

'*Yah!* He is better! *Yah!*'

'*Mbukwa*,' said the man, when the porridge would allow him.

His relatives could not even greet him, so great was their astonishment! We hurried them outside again.

'Huh,' said Daudi. 'And what about his cows now? Two for you, and three for me!'

'Stop,' said a relative. 'Do not say those words! Did we not sin greatly? But how were we to know that he would recover? It's never happened before.'

'If you're sorry, go and tell others that we indeed can cure the disease of death. Get them to come in early so that they, too, can live. Tell what has happened to your own relative.'

Day and night people came in. The staff worked like Trojans. Mika, the clergyman, seemed to be always at the hospital. He would take group after group into his little office, and earnestly draw the parallel between a saved life and a saved soul. He told them of his Master, of Calvary, of the Resurrection, and of a living, personal Saviour. I have never seen a better illustration of medical work being the spearhead for the preaching of the Gospel.

The first fury of the epidemic had died down. It may have been that the staff were becoming a trifle careless, for I had insisted on the most careful precautions being taken by nurses and dressers, to avoid infection. Fewer and fewer cases came to the hospital, and I felt that the staff, at any rate, had avoided it, but imagine my horror when one day a senior nurse fainted on duty, and showed early signs of the disease. She was put to bed at once, the usual minor operation was performed, and the fluid drawn off from her spine. I held the test-tube up to the light and it showed that sinister milkiness that indicated meningitis. Daudi took a couple of drops and smeared them on a glass slide and stained them, and there were those tell-tale germs that looked like two minute french beans, facing one another – the meningococcus – extremely minute, but more death-dealing than all the lions, crocodiles, leopards and poisonous snakes of East Africa.

I had sent Samson to prepare a strong injection of M. & B. He came back to me, with distress written on every feature.

'There are only four pills left in the tin, Bwana!'

'Oh, that'll be all right. The mail comes in today, and I'm expecting some more.'

The mail came in. It consisted of three letters. All told me the same story. No more pills were available in Kenya, Uganda or Tanganyika. East African stocks were finished. I called the staff together, and told them the situation.

'Unless we have these pills by noon tomorrow, Blandina will die.'

'Bwana, did you shake out the mail-bag?' asked old Sechelela.

'I turned it inside out, Mother,' I replied.

'Then there's no way out,' she said. 'Let us pray. This situation is beyond us. Only God can deal with it.'

For a quarter of an hour we knelt, one after the other praying simply, and to the point. They certainly believed that God would answer, but somehow my own faith wavered. We would get no more mail for four days. There was no sign of the package which

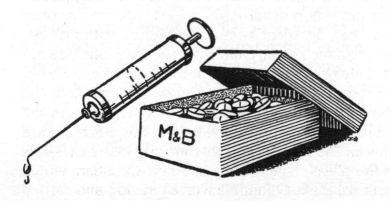

would mean so much to us. It was the wet season. No cars would get through to us over that morass of wet mud. How could we get pills?

I walked home through the dusk, my mind in a turmoil. I ate my dinner, and sat idly turning the pages of an out-of-date newspaper. Timoteyo came in.

'A special messenger brought a parcel for you, Bwana.'

I was expecting a new inner-tube.

'Just put it on the table,' I replied, without looking up.

'Roger hasn't come back yet, Bwana. It's five days since he went away.'

'Oh, I expect he's having difficulty with his relatives. They won't part up with their cows.'

'*Hodi*,' came an urgent voice at the door. 'Bwana, Blandina is delirious.'

I hurried to the ward, and was dismayed to find that her condition had become worse. I gave her an injection of all the remaining tablets, and felt unspeakably miserable as I walked back to the house. Blandina had been little short of heroic at times. I remembered once how she had spent twenty-four hours without rest, looking after a small child with tick-fever. She was not officially on duty, but she felt that only she, with her experience, could steer the child safely through the crisis of the disease. My mind flew to a time when she had run, for six months, the branch hospital ten miles away in the jungle. The witchdoctor had cast spells on the place – spells that, to a non-Christian, would mean death, but Blandina trusted in God and carried on. They had sent armed men, who had beaten on the door at night, and howled to scare the patients. Blandina threw hot water on them! And now, here she was, dying, and we had not enough of the only drug which readily could have saved her. I took up the paper again and despondently finished the article. Then I decided to look at my parcel, hoping that this time they had sent the right sized tube. I unwrapped it, and sprang to my feet in excitement. It was a tin of 500 M. & B. pills, and a note from the Government Doctor, forty miles away:

Dear Doctor,
   We have been sent a double issue of these, and thought perhaps you could find some use for 500.

Could I! I packed the tin under my arm and went for the hospital at the double. They were all sitting round a fire. I was too puffed to speak. They saw the familiar tin.

'*Kah*,' said Daudi, 'they've come! I knew God would answer. Now we can save Blandina.'

In the firelight we knelt and thanked God.

Samson hurried off to light his primus and prepare the pills and syringe.

I went again to the ward. Lying there with her head drawn back was Blandina, raving in delirium, and moaning. Rapidly I gave her another injection.

I saw the other cases, and left instructions. Daudi walked back with me through the shadowy baobabs.

'I knew God would do it, Bwana. If we trust Him, and follow His plans, and obey His will, what else can He do? Is He not our Father?'

'Yes, Daudi, there is no other life worth living, but what many people forget is that we must live our lives on God's terms.'

'That's so. Good night, Bwana.'

We gripped hands.

As I knelt before turning in I thanked God that before we called He had answered. I apologised for my doubts, and somehow I felt my faith was greater.

Next morning, Blandina was definitely easier.

Daudi came to me:

'It's great to see her so much better, Bwana. But have you heard anything of Roger?'

'Not yet, Daudi. I expect he's just cow-hunting.'

'He said he'd be back on Friday, Bwana, and it's not like him to be three days late.'

Nora came up.

'Bwana, has Roger returned?'

'Not yet, Nora. The loafer! I suppose he's having a feast somewhere.'

But she didn't smile. Her eyes were troubled.

'I'm worried, Bwana. I have doubts.'

That evening a messenger arrived from Buigiri. Daudi had seen him from the hospital, and ran down for news. I was just hoeing my forlorn flower-garden. The messenger handed me a letter. I tore it open, and read:

Dear Doctor,

I am writing to tell you that your Roger died of meningitis yesterday, while he was being carried into hospital. He had tried to walk in to us, but collapsed

141

on the way, and when his relatives had finished haggling with the porters over the sum to be paid for his transport, it was too late…

I handed Daudi the letter. The sun had gone behind the hill, and it was rapidly growing dark. I saw a figure hurrying down between the church and the village school. It was Nora. Daudi saw her, too.

'Let me tell her, Bwana.'

But she needed no telling. She looked at us with anguish in her eyes.

'We will see him again, but not in Ugogo,' he said, gently.

Nora was too stunned to reply. She stood quietly for a moment, and then slowly, with head bowed, walked off into the gloom.

I put my hand on Daudi's shoulder. I had no words to fit the situation.

'That's Africa, Bwana. Our Africa.'

Jungle Doctor Series

CHRISTIAN FOCUS PUBLICATIONS

Christian Focus | Christian Heritage | CF4K | Mentor

Christian Focus Publications publishes books for adults and children under its four main imprints: Christian Focus, CF4K, Mentor and Christian Heritage. Our books reflect that God's word is reliable and Jesus is the way to know him, and live for ever with him.

Our children's publication list includes a Sunday School curriculum that covers pre-school to early teens; puzzle and activity books. We also publish personal and family devotional titles, biographies and inspirational stories that children will love.

If you are looking for quality Bible teaching for children then we have an excellent range of Bible story and age specific theological books.

From pre-school to teenage fiction, we have it covered!

Find us at our web page:
www.christianfocus.com

CF4•K
Because you're never too young to know Jesus